MY FEAR OF PUBLIC SPEAKING

ARVIND UPADHYAY

ISBN 979-888530948-6

If you poll a group of people and ask them their greatest fear, public speaking usually ranks number one. In fact, in surveys I have conducted with clients at hundreds of seminars and workshops, 67 percent find public speaking difficult. The remaining 33 percent are comfortable with their public speaking skills but feel there is room for improvement. No matter which percentile you fall into My Fear of Public Speaking will help you assess your speaking skills and learn fast, effective strategies to become a better, more confident public speaker. Throughout my career as a public speaker, I have identified many reasons why people are not comfortable speaking in front of a group, large or small. Some people are self-conscious about their appearance or voice. Others are afraid they will be laughed at or criticized. Such fears can compromise your effectiveness, preventing you from becoming a more confident public speaker. Improving your public speaking and communication skills increases your self-confidence, but studies have revealed an additional benefit: Professionals with good communication skills are promoted more often and faster within their job environment. Top company executives polled said that the one essential skill they look for in an employee slated for promotion is the ability to effectively communicate ideas. Communication is the backbone of our society. It allows us to form connections, influence decisions, and motivate change. Without communication skills, the ability to progress in the working world and in life, itself, would be nearly impossible.

Public speaking is one of the most important and most dreaded forms of communication. Glossophobia or speech anxiety, is the most common fear people have across the globe. Throughout primary school, it is easy to be the student who sits in the back of the classroom and avoids raising his or her hand to dodge such situations. But in the working world, public speaking is a vital skill to have and to hone. It effects simple, everyday interactions between coworkers, bosses and employees, marketing professionals and clients, etc., and it can have an enormous impact on your career path and your level of success in your industry.

To Win Over the Crowd

An important skill to have in business and especially in the public relations arena is the skill of persuasion or the ability to win over the crowd. Inside and outside the workplace, the power of persuasion can carry you far and it all starts by honing those public speaking skills. Mastering public speaking results in an increase in confidence and with that, a cool and collected presence in front of an audience. Of course it is imperative to be knowledgeable about the subject you are presenting, but beyond that, when making a persuasive speech of any kind, including a sales pitch to a client, you need to be prepared to answer the opposition, and to speak with poise.

To make a strong case, the ability to speak publicly is not only important, but essential to make forward strides. For example, in order to express why a certain product or idea would be an interesting topic to an editor of a publication, one must use strong enough, convincing language to elicit intrigue and curiosity. A great pitch will persuade the consumer or editor to want to know more. When addressing any audience with an idea or argument for or against something, public speaking allows you to make your case compellingly and convincingly.

To Motivate People

A great public speaker attains the power to motivate his or her audience to do something, stop doing something, change a behavior, or reach objectives. But to carry an idea forward, you must be able to excite and enliven your peers, employees, coworkers, customers.

Public speakers are leaders who are able to inspire their audience to work harder to achieve their goals. As a public speaker, your role is to influence your listeners and create an environment where everyone walks out ready to roll. You are not merely giving a speech in the attempt to get your audience to take a certain action; speakers are part of the action and can convey their passion and drive. It is not enough to simply know about the issues at hand but to make your audience share your passion. Elections have been won simply because one candidate was a better public speaker than the other. Being knowledgeable is a factor, of course, but more importantly, being able to arouse passion in people through skilled public speaking will motivate your audience to make a move. When people talk about having a voice in the world, they mean having an impact on the world by voicing your thoughts and your knowledge in an exciting way. A mastery of public speaking allows you to relate to the audience and gain their trust. As a skilled public speaker, you become likable and believable, and you will be able to inspire and even entertain the crowd.

To Inform

The ability to inform is one of the most important aspects of public speaking. From presenting research papers and PowerPoint presentations in school to presenting ideas and pitches to your boss or client, informative public speaking is a vital component of a successful career across all work fields. Once you have their attention, a good informative speech sharing your knowledge of a subject with an audience, enhances their understanding and makes them remember your words long after you've finished. For example, you might be asked to instruct a group of coworkers on how to use new computer software or to address your employees on company happenings. Whether it is giving demonstrations or sharing an area of expertise, this form of public speaking is an essential skill in today's world.

According to a study by sociologist, Andrew Zekeri, "Oral communication skills were the number one skill that college graduates found useful in the business world." Communication skills enhance your ability to interact with professionals and fellow colleagues in a qualified and composed manner. Public speaking improves these skills and thus, makes you a more worthy candidate to move up and succeed in your chosen field.

Over ten years ago, I found myself in a class for leaders and managers. After building rapport and working to create a safe environment of trust, the class facilitator decided to have us go around the room and share our insecurities and fears. The coach was specifically homing in on our weaknesses and asking for us to be transparent with others in the room.

As we worked around a small circle, one woman was visibly nervous. When it was her turn, it was as if someone flipped a switch and turned her red. She stumbled over her words as she explained how fearful she was to speak in public. Even in a safe situation with supportive friends, she still was nervous to share. We learned that she even had nightmares where she was in front of a room, perched behind a podium, and she misplaced her notes and looked out at a sea of unforgiving faces. Another attendee encouraged her and told her that she was better off avoiding these events so she didn't trigger her fears.

The fear of public speaking grips many people who avoid it at all costs.

I want to share why this "avoidance thinking" is toxic to aspiring leaders

: No one can learn how to speak who does not first speak as best he can. That may seem like a vicious circle in statement, but it will bear examination. Many teachers have begun with the how. Vain effort! It is an ancient truism that we learn to do by doing. The first thing for the beginner in public speaking is to speak--not to study voice and gesture and the rest. Once he has spoken he can improve himself by self-observation or according to the criticisms of those who hear. But how shall he be able to criticise himself? Simply by finding out three things: What are the qualities which by common consent go to make up an effective speaker; by what means at least some of these qualities may be acquired; and what wrong habits of speech in himself work against his acquiring and using the qualities which he finds to be good. Experience, then, is not only the best teacher, but the first and the last. But experience must be a dual thing--the experience of others must be used to supplement, correct and justify our own experience; in this way we shall become our own best critics only after we have trained ourselves in self-knowledge, the knowledge of what other minds think, and in the ability to judge ourselves by the standards we have come to believe are right. "If I ought," said Kant, "I can." An examination of the contents of this volume will show how consistently these articles of faith have been declared, expounded, and illustrated. The student is urged to begin to speak at once of what he knows. Then he is given simple suggestions for self-control, with gradually increasing emphasis upon the power of the inner man over the outer. Next, the way to the rich storehouses of material is pointed out. And finally, all the while he is urged to speak, speak, SPEAK as he is applying to his own methods, in his own personal way, the principles he has gathered from his own experience and observation and the recorded experiences of others. So now at the very first let it be as clear as light that methods are secondary matters; that the full mind, the warm heart, the dominant will are primary--and not only primary but paramount; for unless it be a full being that uses the methods it will be like dressing a wooden image in the clothes of a man.

Sense never fails to give them that have it, Words enough to make them understood. It too often happens in some conversations, as in Apothecary Shops, that those Pots that are Empty, or have Things of small Value in them, are as gaudily Dress'd as those that are full of precious Drugs. They that soar too high, often fall hard, making a low and level Dwelling preferable. The tallest Trees are most in the Power of the Winds, and Ambitious Men of the Blasts of Fortune. Buildings have need of a good Foundation, that lie so much exposed to the Weather.

Contents

Foreword

Do you feel more comfortable talking on your iphone or on facebook than making a speech in front of others? If your answer is yes, you are not alone. In fact, you may be thinking that with your job and personal life you won't really need to be skilled in public speaking. If so, you will probably view with skepticism my telling you that there are several extremely important reasons for taking a course in public speaking. By the time you finish reading this chapter, I think you will begin to see several personal benefits for learning to give speeches in public. By the time you complete this course, you will be able to say firsthand how learning to give speeches and communicating publicly has benefited you. So let's begin by looking at the potential roles of public speaking in your life, as well as the elements and ethics of the communication process Although you may be thinking that speaking won't be necessary in your life, actually as you become successful in your career, get involved in your community, and pursue various activities and causes, you will be surprised at how many opportunities you will have to give speeches. These opportunities can enhance your personal development, influence society, and advance your career.

Public speaking is a great way of building personal development on many levels, since improving communication skills is helpful in almost every area of life. Whether your goal is to engage in political debate, make a career as a motivational speaker or gain confidence in front of an audience, public speaking can help you meet your goal.

If you expect your audience to pay attention, they must be sufficiently stimulated and motivated. A stimulus triggers and directs attention to your topic; motivation provides a personal benefit that ensures continued audience attention. To illustrate, think about how many times an instructor has asked a question in class, and even though you thought you knew the answer—that is, you were stimulated—you did not respond. Perhaps you were not sufficiently motivated—that is, you saw no personal benefit in answering. Or perhaps you saw a greater benefit in not answering—you were afraid of being criticized by the professor or looking foolish by risking a wrong answer. Of course, if you knew that the professor graded on class participation, your motivation to answer would probably be greater.

Message Encoding and Decoding The process of putting your message into a form that your specific audience will understand is called encoding.

It includes organization of content, language choice, volume, tone of voice, facial expressions, and gestures, to name a few. Careful analysis of your audience is important for effective encoding. When your listeners pick up your message, they try to determine exactly what you mean. This process of interpreting meaning is called decoding. Encoding and decoding are responsible for many of the misunderstandings that occur between speakers and listeners. As a speaker, you use your own frame of reference—your experiences and background—to encode messages. Your listeners, however, use their own frames of reference to decode those messages. Because our frames of reference include our educational background, race, gender, cultural background, hometown, parents, attitudes, personality, and past experiences, no two of us have exactly the same frame of reference.

We've listed the top benefits of public speaking, which will encourage you to get out of your comfort zone and sign up to speak at a few events in the future.

1. Career advancement

Effective public speaking skills can help with career advancement, as they indicate creativity, critical thinking skills, leadership abilities, poise, and professionalism, qualities which are very valuable for the job market.

Speaking at events and conferences is a good way of building credibility. The more well known the event the better, as you can add these speaking achievements to your resume.

Public speaking can also help you stand out at work. You'll learn to speak up in meetings, to promote your ideas, and to present yourself as a professional. Speaking skills can also help you excel in job interviews.

After speaking at a few events, people will remember you and begin to see you as an authoritative figure on your area of expertise. You'll find yourself getting new client and business from people who watched you speak. All sorts of new business and speaking opportunities will open up for you.

2. Boost confidence

Public speaking can significantly boost your confidence. Overcoming the fears and insecurities that accompany public speaking is empowering. Furthermore, connecting with audiences can be a strong reminder that you have valuable insights and opinions to share with the world.

Your confidence levels will grow as you go from speaking to small groups of people up to large audiences. This will benefit you not just on stage, but in everyday life as well, whether it be in a meeting or on a date.

A study by North Carolina Cooperative Extension of people aged 9 to 18 who participated in a public speaking program found that public speaking increased confidence. The study found that meeting a goal was an important factor when it came to increasing the students confidence.

While the nervousness that comes with speaking in front of a crowd won't entirely disappear, it will teach you how to deal with your fears and turn your weakness into strength.

3. Critical thinking

Public speaking is an excellent way to build critical thinking skills. Writing a speech requires a great deal of careful thought, from the audience analysis to the closing sentence. It's not enough to have a message, you also need to figure out how to tailor the message to fit the needs of your audience.

How can you make your points relevant to your listeners? How can you help the audience understand your views? If you start thinking critically about your speaking style, you may find ways to improve your general communication style at home and at work.

4. Personal development

Communication skills are crucial for personal and professional success and improving this area is one of the greatest benefits of public speaking. Preparing a speech forces speakers to take a step back and think critically about effective ways to communicate. In everyday life, it's easy to fall back on communication habits we formed many years ago.

5. Improve communication skills

When you write a speech, you have to think carefully about the best framework, persuasive strategy, and diction to communicate your message to the audience. This type of thinking can help you improve your communication skills in other areas of your life.

Personal relationships, social interactions and work situations require you to communicate ideas to other people. Public speaking focuses on communicating ideas. You can learn to calmly take up an opposing view, to present your ideas in an organized and coherent manner, and to defend your views to others.

6. Make new social connections

Public speaking engagements are good places to meet other people who share your interests. You'll find that people approach you after your presentation to engage in conversation. It makes it much easier to make new social connections. Try to mingle with the audience for as long as you can after your speech, answering questions and seeking fresh perspectives on your topic.

Give audience members the option of getting in touch with you at a later date by listing contact information on handouts or slides. If you have a website, direct audience members to find more information there.

If you are part of a speaking line-up, reach out to your fellow presenters. Congratulate them or, if you miss a talk, ask how it went. There are lots of opportunities for networking in the realm of public speaking, so plan ahead and make use of them.

7. Personal satisfaction

Public speaking is a very common phobia, right up there with spiders and heights. Many people would prefer to do almost anything instead of standing up and talking in front a crowd of people. Delivering a speech can feel intimidating and risky.

Fears and insecurities tend to multiply as the speech draws closer: "What if I forget my speech?" "What if I can't answer the audience's questions?" Public speaking is a way of showing yourself that, with practice, you can do the things that scare you the most. What starts out as a nightmare can turn into a personal boost.

8. Expand your professional network

Another benefit of public speaking is that when you speak at an event, you will suddenly find that everyone wants to talk with you. This is a valuable opportunity for making friends, building business contacts and generating business.

Not only this, but you also get the opportunity to network with other speakers, some of whom may be very difficult to contact normally. Speaking events may also have guest rooms for speakers where they are given food and drink and can network together.

9. Learn to persuade

Public speaking has a long history as a catalyst for nonviolent activism and political change. It is a powerful way to unite people under a common cause and motivate them to take action. It's no secret that people throughout history have used the power of public speaking to make a difference.

You'll hardly ever have a better opportunity to speak to a captive audience about what really matters to you. You'll get a chance to influence your peers. You won't change the world with every speech, but you can easily impact someone in some small way.

10. Build leadership skills

If you let others do your talking for you in the past or found it hard to express what you wanted to say, that will fade. Not only will you be able to fluently speak your mind but you'll find yourself doing it for others too.

In standing up and speaking in a way that is powerful, you're speaking in a way that will change people's minds about something. If you're able to master that skill, changing hearts and minds and learning how to persuade, you will be already honing one of the major aspects of leadership.

If you're able to do it in public to a group of people, chances are you'll be able to do it in a more individualized setting. Leaders require the capacity to drive change, public speaking skills are vital in learning that ability.

11. Learn performance skills

You'll have become conscious of timing, when to pause and how long for. You'll know about vocal variety, how to shift through changes of volume, speech rate and tone. Your articulation will be clearer. As you become more confident you'll know about mime, using props and storytelling. All of these acting skills enhance your speech.

12. Develop your vocabulary and fluency

You'll know the effect of the words you choose to express your message and you'll also know they need to be different for different audiences. As well as having a flexible vocabulary, you'll no longer use common filler words we hear in everyday conversation indicating that the speaker may be unsure about what they're saying or anxious about speaking.

13. No fear of impromptu speaking

When called upon to say a few words at a moment's notice at a wedding, awards ceremony or other special occasion, your heart will not pound. Instead you'll find yourself graciously accepting the opportunity for an impromptu speech. This is a huge benefit of public speaking and you'll stop constantly worrying at formal events about being asked to speak.

14. Learn to argue

When you present, you often need to put forward a well thought out argument. In the preparation, in the practice and on the actual stage, you will learn much about the art of argument, especially if you get to engage with your audience in some form of question and answer.

15. Helps you drive change

Who do we listen to more, someone talking to us in person or an email? The person speaking is always going to be more convincing than a note sent across the internet. You could spend your time going from person to person, if that's your comfort zone.

But think about how many more people you could reach if you stood up on stage and had them all gathered together in an audience. If you're speaking to an audience of 300 versus one-on-one, then you're driving serious change. The more people you're able to speak to, the more change you can implement.

16. Be a better listener

Listening may be a lost art, but a public speaking course actually teaches you to become a better listener. When you attend conferences, you'll hear several different types of speeches about a wide variety of topics, from people who may be very different from you. This will passively build your listening ability and note taking.

These benefits of public speaking make getting out of your comfort zone and giving a speech absolutely worth it. You'll be nervous the first few times you speak, however you'll quickly learn to enjoy the experience.

Preface

The most successful model for teaching public speaking (and the one this classfollows) relies on a mix of instruction, imitation, and practice. • Instruction reinforces the lessons learned from the history of public speaking study. The instruction in this class draws most explicitly from the rhetorical tradition. We will study principles of argumentation, arrangement, and style. • Imitation means that when studying a performance skill like speaking, we benefit by identifying and imitating the best practices of skilled speakers. I don't mean stealing or plagiarizing, I mean trying to link phrasestogether in a mannersimilar to a speaker we think sounds good. There are a number of speeches that you will watch during this course (online and in class). The intent of these speeches is to show you some best practices. You shouldn't simply watch a speech like you would a television show; you should look to find some verbal or nonverbal behaviorsthat you would like to be able to imitate. • Practice isthe most obviousleg of public speaking study. If you are going to get better at public speaking, you must be able to apply the lessons of instruction and imitation by practicing your speeches. The nice thing about public speaking is that you can practice it almost anywhere. However, your practice time is best spent by speaking in situations where you have an attentive audience (as opposed to a curious dog or a sleeping roommate).

MISCONCEPTIONS ABOUT PUBLIC SPEAKING 1 You can't learn to be a good public speaker; you have to be born a naturally good speaker. Everyone can become a better public speaker through study and practice. I love to ski. I wasn't born a good skier; rather, I grew up skiing. I skied as often as I could, and I got better. The same istrue of public speaking. You were born with the basic equipment needed for speaking in public—lungs and a mouth. 2 I can only learn public speaking through practice. This misconception often works in conjunction with the misconception #1 and #3. I see this as a hugely egoistic argument since it assumes that only you know what good public speaking is and only you know how to improve. Let me return to the skiing analogy (though you could substitute any sports or skills analogy, like playing a musical instrument). Most people develop their skiing ability by simply skiing a lot. But if you want to get better, you need to seek outside information about the principles of skiing. That's why people pay a lot of money for ski lessons. Ski instructors can both model good skiing behaviors and they can talk about the physics of metal on snow and the physiology of your muscles on skis. 3 Public speaking isjust delivery (speech content doesn't matter). Thisislike saying that a good essay is simply one that has good grammar or punctuation. A good essay should have good grammar and punctuation, but it also needs good content. The same holdstrue of a speech. When we listen to a speech we judge the speaker according to what they say as well as how they say it. Think about presidential debates. After any presidential debate, pundits flood the airwaves and pick apart both content and delivery, but they spend far more time discussing what the candidates said. 4 Reading a speech isthe best way to ensure a good speech. You will hear me talking a lot about the similarities between writing and speaking, but they also differ in many important respects. A speech is an act of communication with a specific audience. Reading a speech underminesthis (and as we will see, can actually make you more nervous). If you were having a conversation with a friend about your classes and suddenly started reading a prepared set of comments, the conversation would sink. Why? A conversation is dynamic and relies on communicating with the other person. A speech is like a conversation in this way, you are engaging in a shared act of communication with the audience. As you can see, strong public speaking skills is not something that people are born with or something that we can do alone. Now that you have an idea of what to expect from this course, what is expected of you, and why public speaking is vitally important, lets get started!

Public speaking is a common form of anxiety and fear. Over 75% of people experience some degree of anxiety or nervousness when it comes to speaking in front of others. People who have been surveyed commonly rank this fear above spiders, heights, and death. So, the first thing to remember is that your fear is totally normal. It can range from slight nervousness to paralyzing fear and panic, with more extreme fear known as glossophobia. Many people with this fear avoid public speaking situations altogether, or they suffer through them with shaking hands and a quavering voice. But with preparation and experience, you can overcome your fear.GLOSSOPHOBIA: MORE THAN A COMMON FEAR OF SPEAKING Most of us have experienced some sort of fear when speaking in public. However, a person with glossophobia is unable to control their nerves and has an extremely strong fear of public speaking, sometimes to the point of a nervous breakdown. With this can come uncontrollable trembling, sweating, and a racing heartbeat. This anxiety may not be confined to speaking to large audiences – people suffering with glossophobia may struggle to speak in a meeting, classroom, and other smaller group settings. This can make it very difficult for sufferers to communicate verbally in order to express their ideas and thoughts. As a result, glossophobia may hamper the sufferer's ability to further his or her academic, social or career opportunities.

Prologue

Frame your story There's no way you can give a good talk unless you have something worth talking about. Conceptualizing and framing what you want to say is the most vital part of preparation. We all know that stories are a powerful tool for communication and therefore, metaphors which abound the narrative structures work best to engage people. Approach 1: Consider it as planning a journey where the biggest decisions are where to start and where to end. To find the right place to start, consider what people in the audience already know about your subject – and how much they care about it. If you assume they have more knowledge or interest than they in fact do, or if you start using jargon or get too technical, you'll lose them. The most engaging speakers do a superb job of very quickly introducing the topic, explaining why they care so deeply about it, and convincing the audience members that they should, too. Approach 2: Have a narrative structure that loosely follows a detective story. The speaker starts out by presenting a problem and then describes the search for a solution. There's an "aha" moment, and the audience's perspective shifts in a meaningful way. As a general rule, people are not very interested in talks about organizations or institutions. Ideas and stories fascinate us; organizations bore us – they're much harder to relate to. The take-away message If someone who missed your talk were to ask an audience member in the elevator to sum it up, what would you like that person to say? Focus on that message. Start out with this summary statement in mind and build your presentation around it. Plan your delivery There are three main ways to deliver a speech. You can read it directly off a script. You can develop a set of bullet points that map out what you're going to say in each section rather than scripting the whole thing word for word. Or you can memorize your speech, which entails rehearsing it to the point where you internalize every word. Don't do number one as reading a speech is the most boring thing for everyone! For me bullet points proved to be the most reasonable system as remembering the entire speech by heart might prove too stressful or time-consuming. Don't write out the material word-by-word and don't plan on reading text even if you do have it all written down. Having the text written out and parts of it memorized will constrain you. Memorize the structure of the talk and the outline, but not every word. Timing People rarely want to listen to someone for longer than the allotted time. Few people are such amazing speakers that an audience can't get enough of them. Do not assume you are one of those few. Wrap up your talk on time. To achieve this goal, ask someone to give you time cues by indicating when you have five minutes left, two minutes and when you have run out of time. Once you get the last notice, you should stop talking. Take a really long time to explain what your talk is about. Speak slowly and dramatically. Why talk when you can orate? Make sure you subtly let everyone know how important you are. Refer to your book repeatedly. Even better, quote yourself from it. Speak at great length about the history of your organization and its glorious achievements. Use lots of unexplained technical jargon to make yourself sound smart. Cram your slides with numerous text bullet points and multiple fonts. Don't bother rehearsing to check how long your talk is running. Never, ever make eye contact with anyone in the audience Sound as if you're reciting your talk from memory. 10 WAYS TO RUIN A PRESENTATION Flexibility Organize your talk and know it well enough to have the flexibility to skip certain parts or expand on others depending on the circumstances. For example, if you do add a last-minute introduction, be flexible to skip a part of the prepared content. Practice makes perfect Practice the presentation a few times: more if you have less experience, less if you are a more seasoned public speaker. It can be especially helpful to give the talk to someone who is not in your field and is not intimately familiar with the material. This is helpful in seeing whether you have made the talk too narrowly focused or overly technical. Such a practice session does not have to involve the entire talk, it can consist of telling someone about your presentation outline.

CHAPTER ONE

CONFIDENCE BEFORE AN AUDIENCE

There is a strange sensation often experienced in the presence of an audience. It may proceed from the gaze of the many eyes that turn upon the speaker, especially if he permits himself to steadily return that gaze. Most speakers have been conscious of this in a nameless thrill, a real something, pervading the atmosphere, tangible, evanescent, indescribable. All writers have borne testimony to the power of a speaker's eye in impressing an audience. This influence which we are now considering is the reverse of that picture--the power their eyes may exert upon him, especially before he begins to speak: after the inward fires of oratory are fanned into flame the eyes of the audience lose all terror. --WILLIAM PITTENGER, Extempore Speech. Students of public speaking continually ask, "How can I overcome self-consciousness and the fear that paralyzes me before an audience?" Did you ever notice in looking from a train window that some horses feed near the track and never even pause to look up at the thundering cars, while just ahead at the next railroad crossing a farmer's wife will be nervously trying to quiet her scared horse as the train goes by? How would you cure a horse that is afraid of cars--graze him in a back-woods lot where he would never see steam-engines or automobiles, or drive or pasture him where he would frequently see the machines? Apply horse-sense to ridding yourself of self-consciousness and fear: face an audience as frequently as you can, and you will soon stop shying. You can never attain freedom from stage-fright by reading a treatise. A book may give you excellent suggestions on how best to conduct yourself in the water, but sooner or later you must get wet, perhaps even strangle and be "half scared to death." There are a great many "wetless" bathing suits worn at the seashore, but no one ever learns to swim in them. To plunge is the only way. Practise, practise, PRACTISE in speaking before an audience will tend to remove all fear of audiences, just as practise in swimming will lead to confidence and facility in the water. You must learn to speak by speaking. The Apostle Paul tells us that every man must work out his own salvation. All we can do here is to offer you suggestions as to how best to prepare for your plunge. The real plunge no one can take for you. A doctor may prescribe, but you must take the medicine. Do not be disheartened if at first you suffer from stage-fright. Dan Patch was more susceptible to suffering than a superannuated dray horse would be. It never hurts a fool to appear before an audience, for his capacity is not a capacity for feeling. A blow that would kill a civilized man soon heals on a savage. The higher we go in the scale of life, the greater is the capacity for suffering. For one reason or another, some master-speakers never entirely overcome stage-fright, but it will pay you to spare no pains to conquer it. Daniel Webster failed in his first appearance and had to take his seat without finishing his speech because he was nervous. Gladstone was often troubled with self-consciousness in the beginning of an address. Beecher was always perturbed before talking in public. Blacksmiths sometimes twist a rope tight around the nose of a horse, and by thus inflicting a little pain they distract his attention from the shoeing process. One way to get air out of a glass is to pour in water. Be Absorbed by Your Subject CHAPTER I 7 Apply the blacksmith's homely principle when you are speaking. If you feel deeply about your subject you will be able to think of little else. Concentration is a process of distraction from less important matters. It is too late to think about the cut of your coat when once you are upon the platform, so centre your interest on what you are about to say--fill your mind with your speech-material and, like the infilling water in the glass, it will drive out your unsubstantial fears. Self-consciousness is undue consciousness of self, and, for the purpose of delivery, self is secondary to your subject, not only in the opinion of the audience, but, if you are wise, in your own. To hold any other view is to regard yourself as an exhibit instead of as a messenger with a message worth delivering. Do you remember Elbert Hubbard's tremendous little tract, "A Message to Garcia"? The youth subordinated himself to the message he bore. So must you, by all the determination you can muster. It is sheer egotism to fill your mind with thoughts of self when a greater thing is there--TRUTH. Say this to yourself sternly, and shame your self-consciousness into quiescence. If the theater caught fire you could rush to the stage and shout directions to the audience without any self-consciousness, for the importance of what you were saying would drive all fear-thoughts out of your mind. Far worse than self-consciousness through fear of doing poorly is self-consciousness through assumption of doing well. The first sign of greatness is when a man does not attempt to look and act great. Before you can call yourself a man at all, Kipling assures us, you must "not look too good nor talk too wise." Nothing advertises itself so thoroughly as conceit. One may be so full of self as to be empty. Voltaire said, "We must conceal self-love." But that can not be done. You know this to be true, for you have recognized overweening self-love in others. If you have it, others are seeing it in you. There are things in this world bigger than self, and in working for them self will be forgotten, or--what is better--remembered only so as to help us win toward higher things. Have Something to Say The trouble with many speakers is that they go before an audience with their minds a blank. It is no wonder that nature, abhorring a vacuum, fills them with the nearest thing handy, which generally happens to be, "I wonder if I am doing this right! How does my hair look? I know I shall fail." Their prophetic souls are sure to be right. It is not enough to be absorbed by your subject--to acquire self-confidence you must have something in which to be confident. If you go before an audience without any preparation, or previous knowledge of your subject, you ought to be self-conscious--you ought to be ashamed to steal the time of your audience. Prepare yourself. Know what you are going to talk about, and, in general, how you are going to say it. Have the first few sentences worked out completely so that you may not be troubled in the beginning to find words. Know your subject better than your hearers know it, and you have nothing to fear. After Preparing for Success, Expect It Let your bearing be modestly confident, but most of all be modestly confident within. Over-confidence is bad, but to tolerate premonitions of failure is worse, for a bold man may win attention by his very bearing, while a rabbit-hearted coward invites disaster. Humility is not the personal discount that we must offer in the presence of others--against this old interpretation there has been a most healthy modern reaction. True humility any man who thoroughly knows himself must feel; but it is not a humility that assumes a worm-like meekness; it is rather a strong, vibrant prayer for greater power for service--a prayer that Uriah Heep could never have uttered. Washington Irving once introduced Charles Dickens at a dinner given in the latter's honor. In the middle of his speech Irving hesitated, became embarrassed, and sat down awkwardly. Turning to a friend beside him he remarked, "There, I told you I would fail, and I did." If you believe you will fail, there is no hope for you. You will.

Rid yourself of this I-am-a-poor-worm-in-the-dust idea. You are a god, with infinite capabilities. "All things are ready if the mind be so." The eagle looks the cloudless sun in the face. Assume Mastery Over Your Audience In public speech, as in electricity, there is a positive and a negative force. Either you or your audience are going to possess the positive factor. If you assume it you can almost invariably make it yours. If you assume the negative you are sure to be negative. Assuming a virtue or a vice vitalizes it. Summon all your power of self-direction, and remember that though your audience is infinitely more important than you, the truth is more important than both of you, because it is eternal. If your mind falters in its leadership the sword will drop from your hands. Your assumption of being able to instruct or lead or inspire a multitude or even a small group of people may appall you as being colossal impudence--as indeed it may be; but having once essayed to speak, be courageous. BE courageous--it lies within you to be what you will. MAKE yourself be calm and confident. Reflect that your audience will not hurt you. If Beecher in Liverpool had spoken behind a wire screen he would have invited the audience to throw the over-ripe missiles with which they were loaded; but he was a man, confronted his hostile hearers fearlessly--and won them. In facing your audience, pause a moment and look them over--a hundred chances to one they want you to succeed, for what man is so foolish as to spend his time, perhaps his money, in the hope that you will waste his investment by talking dully? Concluding Hints Do not make haste to begin--haste shows lack of control. Do not apologize. It ought not to be necessary; and if it is, it will not help. Go straight ahead. Take a deep breath, relax, and begin in a quiet conversational tone as though you were speaking to one large friend. You will not find it half so bad as you imagined; really, it is like taking a cold plunge: after you are in, the water is fine. In fact, having spoken a few times you will even anticipate the plunge with exhilaration. To stand before an audience and make them think your thoughts after you is one of the greatest pleasures you can ever know. Instead of fearing it, you ought to be as anxious as the fox hounds straining at their leashes, or the race horses tugging at their reins. So cast out fear, for fear is cowardly--when it is not mastered. The bravest know fear, but they do not yield to it. Face your audience pluckily--if your knees quake, MAKE them stop. In your audience lies some victory for you and the cause you represent. Go win it. Suppose Charles Martell had been afraid to hammer the Saracen at Tours; suppose Columbus had feared to venture out into the unknown West; suppose our forefathers had been too timid to oppose the tyranny of George the Third; suppose that any man who ever did anything worth while had been a coward! The world owes its progress to the men who have dared, and you must dare to speak the effective word that is in your heart to speak--for often it requires courage to utter a single sentence. But remember that men erect no monuments and weave no laurels for those who fear to do what they can. Is all this unsympathetic, do you say?Man, what you need is not sympathy, but a push. No one doubts that temperament and nerves and illness and even praiseworthy modesty may, singly or combined, cause the speaker's cheek to blanch before an audience, but neither can any one doubt that coddling will magnify this weakness. The victory lies in a fearless frame of mind. Prof. Walter Dill Scott says: "Success or failure in business is caused more by mental attitude even than by mental capacity." Banish the fear-attitude; acquire the confident attitude. And remember that the only way to acquire it is--to acquire it.For as long as I can remember, I always think back to when I was only five years old. I would spend the day outside either playing in the dirt or building. At the end of the day I would talk my parents' ears off (I assumed they were listening) about what I built or what I was going to build. Little did I realize that my training as an engineer—my first career—was already beginning. Regardless of your profession, you probably spent your school years training, learning, and fine-tuning your reading and writing skills. If you are like most, you spent very little time learning how to develop your public speaking skills— schools don't typically teach these skills, unless you join the debate team. However, as you will learn shortly, most communications occur on a verbal basis. Each day presents opportunities for informal and formal public speaking, from making a phone call at work to giving a new business presentation or running a meeting. It is a common misconception that certain people are born good speakers. Yes, I agree that some people have the gift of gab—I could think of a few who have too much of a gift— and seem more natural at it. But make no mistake: Becoming a confident public speaker is achieved only by the desire to become a better speaker, followed by focused effort and a lot of practice. The good news is, your payoff will come quickly, you'll have fun along the way, and the confidence you develop will improve virtually all areas of your life. Professional speakers, myself included, never stop practicing and honing their speaking skills. I am a better speaker today than I was five years ago and expect to continue to improve. If you are like most people, you did not have a great firsttime public speaking experience, and the thought of speaking in front of people scares you to death. In fact, according to the Book of Lists, public speaking is the greatest of all fears. More than 41 percent of people polled for the book named public speaking as their number one fear. The fear of dying is number seven on the list! I guess that means people would rather die than get up in front of a group of people to speak. If you feel this way, you're not alone. In fact, some of today's most famous presenters have freely admitted to nervousness and stage fright when it comes to public speaking. You may be saying to yourself right now, There is no way I will be a good speaker. I can never learn to be like those professional speakers; speaking just comes easily to them. Most of us naturally worry about what other people think about us, and this is especially true when we are asked to speak to a group of people. Learning specific techniques to improve your public speaking can help eradicate your fear and help you succeed in your business and personal life.

Whether you are having a casual telephone conversation, teaching a Sunday school class, having a conversation with your boss, or giving a formal presentation, you are involved in public speaking. Following are examples of how public speaking can positively influence your everyday life, your career, your relationships, your communication style, and much more. Let's get started on the path to successful public speaking. • Build success in your professional life. Most presidents and CEOs of companies possess strong speaking skills. I work with many high-level executives in the business world, and when I ask them why they feel they need coaching to improve their speaking skills, they all indicate that they know their success and their companies' future business ventures rely on their ability to speak well. Their promotions to the top were related directly to their ability to communicate effectively. • Communicate with others more clearly. Many mistakes or misinterpretations are a result of not properly communicating your ideas. Good public speaking skills help you articulate ideas well and make them come alive for the listener. This was one of the most critical skills I needed to develop as an engineer, because I often had to speak to audiences that didn't know the first thing about how to "shore up" a building, for example, but had the authority and the money to fund my next project. If I was ineffective in conveying why they should invest more money, I might have been out of a job. • Build overall confidence. As you become better at organizing and communicating your ideas effectively, you will start to exhibit more confidence. People with this ability have a "glow" of confidence when they speak in public. (Let's not confuse this with the red glow of terror on the face of someone who is scared to death.)

• Increase your comfort level in social situations. How many of you have ever been invited to a party and are afraid to strike up a conversation? (Don't be shy, no one can see you.) Social situations are, in fact, the perfect opportunity to practice your public speaking skills. Here's a little bonus: It is a known fact that people who speak well are perceived as better looking. Thank God, now I know why I worked so hard at it, and it wasn't just my cute smile that made me popular with the girls. • Speak more confidently on the telephone. Whether you call to request information, make a cold call at work, communicate with a client, or just leave a phone message, others can hear your confidence level in the tone of your voice. Did you know that over 86 percent of your telephone message is communicated through the tone of your voice? • Run meetings or present new ideas more effectively. I remember running my son's Cub Scout pack. Having the ability to conduct a Cub Scout meeting with six to eight screaming, energetic boys definitely challenged my public speaking skills (and required a lot of aspirin). Organizing and running a meeting with adults is more difficult, I think, because you can't bribe them with candy At some point in your life, you may volunteer or even be affectionately coerced to lead or participate in a professional or social organization. Your success within the organization depends significantly on your ability to speak to a group and keep their attention engaged in order to achieve common goals and objectives. Your success in dealing with clients—or even your own children—depends a great deal on your speaking skills. The ability to convince people with words is key to establishing trust and respect. This can include not only what you say, but how you say it.

There is no magic formula for becoming a polished public speaker. Those of you who play a musical instrument know you do not become proficient without practice. I used to roll my eyes when my mom told me to practice for an hour after school before I went outside. I later came to appreciate that time, and I continued to improve. As a semiprofessional musician (my kids may beg to differ) who has learned to play the guitar and piano, I know what steps I had to take to play these instruments well. It has been said, "To learn to play the trumpet, you have to play the trumpet." Similarly, "To learn to speak, you have to speak." You cannot become an effective communicator by just watching other great speakers. You cannot become a confident public speaker without practice, practice, and even more practice. Many of you have probably heard the two-line cliché "How do you get to Carnegie Hall?" (Answer:) "Practice, practice, practice." Public speaking demands the same level of practice. You can start right away by practicing your public speaking skills in everyday situations.

A terrific first step to developing speaking skills is to begin to focus on how you speak in everyday speaking situations. Let's take a look at four situations where you can begin to polish your speaking skills.

How many of you have bumped into a friend while shopping or running an errand? Here you are—another opportunity to practice your public speaking. • Initiate the conversation. • Ask the person how her family is doing. What's new with her job? Does she have any vacation plans coming up? • Tell a funny story about something that happened recently to you, your family, or your friends. • Think about how fast you speak, how you pronounce your words, and how you organize your thoughts. This is called your natural speaking style and will come in handy later. Parties Parties are the perfect opportunity to practice your public speaking skills. So the next party you attend, make sure you bring your bag of tricks. • If you find yourself standing alone in a corner of the room, don't just eat all the crab dip: Initiate a conversation with the next person who walks by. • Introduce yourself to two new people (see "Your First Speech: 'Introducing Yourself' " later in this chapter). • Participate in a group discussion, but do not dominate the conversation. • Have a conversation with someone you have not seen in a while.

Leaving a Telephone Message

Doesn't it seem nowadays that you leave a message or voice mail more often than reaching someone on the phone right off the bat? Telephone tag is the new corporate sport. Consider these moments golden opportunities to practice your speaking and organization skills. The next time you need to call someone, write a few brief notes so you won't forget anything if you get the person's voice mail—and I guarantee you, you will get their voice mail. • Slow down! Do not speak fast when you are leaving a message, especially if you have an accent. Most answering machines today allow enough time for a short message. I can't tell you the number of messages I get a day where I cannot understand what the caller is saying because he or she is speaking too fast. I often find myself replaying the message a few times. This is why notes come in handy. Also, slow down when saying your telephone number. • Pronounce your name clearly. State your name slowly, especially if your name is not as common as Smith or Jones. Also spell your name slowly if necessary (f as in Friday, t as in ticket . . .). • In addition to your name, give your title, your company name, and the reason you are calling. Describe to the person, in a few short sentences, the purpose of the call. If appropriate, leave the time you called (be sensitive to different time zones). • Let them know when to return the call. Leave a date, preferred time, and telephone number. • Always sound professional. Do not chew gum, and do not leave a long-winded message. Be aware of your tone.

I always tell people to smile when leaving a message—it automatically gives your voice an upbeat, pleasant tone. Should the person you are calling actually answer the telephone, you can still use your notes. It will make you sound professional and organized.

Creating a Voice Messages

Even though you may not have thought about it this way, your own voice mail message is like a little presentation to the public and leaves a first impression. • Before you record your greeting, write it down and practice saying it. Record the message, play it back, and rerecord it if necessary. Is your message too fast? Is it too slow? Is your voice clear and easy to understand? This is great practice for when you prepare your own speech. • Make sure your answering machine greeting sounds professional and friendly. Call your own phone number and listen to your own greeting. Ask yourself if your voice is clear and your message makes sense. You would be surprised at the number of poor greetings I've heard when returning calls. • Leave the caller clear instructions on what to do when leaving a message. • If you run a business, as I do, your voice mail greeting is a great opportunity to plug your business. Be careful of information overload, though.

Calming Your Anxiety

The best way to deal with speaking anxiety is to first acknowledge that this fear is perfectly normal and you are not alone. Most studies suggest fear of public speaking is associated with a stressful childhood or early school year experience speaking in front of others. My fears were limited mostly to being beaten up by the school bully. Most people remember a specific moment in their life when they first experienced this anxiety. It may have been during one of those "show and tell" moments in school when the entire class, especially that girl or boy you had a crush on, laughed at you. We have a tendency to forget why they laughed and just remember that they did! Most people develop speaking phobias while in middle school. This is the time when a well-meaning teacher asked you to speak in front of your class or asked you to say something in a social setting. Yet think about it.

Adolescence is one of the most difficult periods in life. As a middle school student, you were going through tremendous social, emotional, and physical changes and were very sensitive to what other people thought about you, especially your fellow classmates. Unfortunately, many people carry these turbulent feelings into adulthood; thus experiences, good or bad, are etched in your mind forever. You see, it is this fear of failure that you find yourself dealing with at one time in your life. I remember back in middle school when my best friend, Jerry, was going to talk to the entire sixth-grade class about what it is like to play drums. Jerry had made special arrangements to get into the school early so he could set up his drum set. He set up his drums quickly and was ready. When he rushed to his first-period class, he did not see his drum set. He thought someone had played a trick on him and moved it. Jerry was so nervous when he got to school, he had set up his drum set in a similar classroom on the third floor. The problem was, our classroom was on the second floor. He forgot to check which room he was really in. Needless to say, Jerry learned a good lesson. Half of a speaker's or performer's success is just showing up in the right place at the right time. Hopefully something like this has never happened to you. Many people today who work in front of the public, such as singers, actors, and politicians, still experience, to varying degrees, these same fears. Some people call speech anxiety "stage fright." I like to think of it as "speech excitement." How you deal with it starts with what you call it. Speech excitement means positive energy. When I survey the participants in my seminars and probe further, I find similar stories to Jerry's. You'd think I was a doctor asking about their symptoms so I can prescribe the "magic pill" to help them.

Another great technique, which you can use in conjunction with deep breathing, is "visualization." This is a simple process. 1. Close your eyes and imagine, or "visualize," yourself speaking.

2. Picture yourself speaking in a loud, clear, and assured voice, and imagine that the audience is fascinated by what you're saying. Studies have shown that if you visualize yourself giving a successful presentation, you will be successful. Professional and Olympic skiers use visualization, too. Before they actually head down the slope, they visualize in their mind where the gates and turns are and virtually practice the course in their mind. As a professional speaker, I use visualization all the time, visualizing and "navigating" the "course" of a speech before starting. I first visualize myself walking up to the stage as I am introduced and the audience

applauding as I make my way to the podium. It is not unusual for me to arrive early to physically practice walking on stage so later my visualization process is more realistic. Some experts even suggest imagining your audience sitting nude. I don't know about you, but if I tried this with some of my previous audiences, I might get very distracted. The most important part of the visualization process is to think positive.

Positive self-talk is the process of associating a situation with positive results. Imagine people applauding you, not running away, as you walk on stage. Imagine your audience listening to every word you say, not snoring so loudly that even you can't hear yourself. The power of the mind is truly amazing, and those who have a positive outlook experience success, which in turn builds confidence. Don't worry if you have trouble at first. These breathing and visualization techniques take some practice and become easier the more frequently you practice. Try all these tech niques to discover which technique or combination of techniques works best for you.

I, as well as many other professional speakers, all have "warmup" routines. For me, it's arriving early and walking around the room where I will speak. As I said earlier, I walk to the podium or stage and even walk around the room where the audience will be sitting so I can get a feel for the room. Then I find a quiet location, out of sight from the audience, where I practice deep breathing exercises while visualizing the speaking environment. I also visualize people looking at me as my introduction is being given. As I start my speech, I like to smile at the audience and focus on my opening lines. I use this warm-up routine before each speaking engagement. It has the greatest positive effect on me—I not only relax, but I find I actually have more energy. Find a warm-up routine that works for you and begin using it regularly

CHAPTER TWO

SIN OF MONOTONY & GREAT PRESENTATION

Our English has changed with the years so that many words now connote more than they did originally. This is true of the word monotonous. From "having but one tone," it has come to mean more broadly, "lack of variation." The monotonous speaker not only drones along in the same volume and pitch of tone but uses always the same emphasis, the same speed, the same thoughts--or dispenses with thought altogether. Monotony, the cardinal and most common sin of the public speaker, is not a transgression--it is rather a sin of omission, for it consists in living up to the confession of the Prayer Book: "We have left undone those things we ought to have done." Emerson says, "The virtue of art lies in detachment, in sequestering one object from the embarrassing variety." That is just what the monotonous speaker fails to do--he does not detach one thought or phrase from another, they are all expressed in the same manner. To tell you that your speech is monotonous may mean very little to you, so let us look at the nature--and the curse--of monotony in other spheres of life, then we shall appreciate more fully how it will blight an otherwise good speech. If the Victrola in the adjoining apartment grinds out just three selections over and over again, it is pretty safe to assume that your neighbor has no other records. If a speaker uses only a few of his powers, it points very plainly to the fact that the rest of his powers are not developed. Monotony reveals our limitations. In its effect on its victim, monotony is actually deadly--it will drive the bloom from the cheek and the lustre from the eye as quickly as sin, and often leads to viciousness. The worst punishment that human ingenuity has ever been able to invent is extreme monotony--solitary confinement. Lay a marble on the table and do nothing eighteen hours of the day but change that marble from one point to another and back again, and you will go insane if you continue long enough. So this thing that shortens life, and is used as the most cruel of punishments in our prisons, is the thing that will destroy all the life and force of a speech. Avoid it as you would shun a deadly dull bore. The "idle rich" can have half-a-dozen homes, command all the varieties of foods gathered from the four corners of the earth, and sail for Africa or Alaska at their pleasure; but the poverty-stricken man must walk or take a street car--he does not have the choice of yacht, auto, or special train. He must spend the most of his life in labor and be content with the staples of the food-market. Monotony is poverty, whether in speech or in life. Strive to increase the variety of your speech as the business man labors to augment his wealth. Bird-songs, forest glens, and mountains are not monotonous--it is the long rows of brown-stone fronts and the miles of paved streets that are so terribly same. Nature in her wealth gives us endless variety; man with his limitations is often monotonous. Get back to nature in your methods of speech-making. The power of variety lies in its pleasure-giving quality. The great truths of the world have often been couched in fascinating stories--"Les Miserables," for instance. If you wish to teach or influence men, you must please them, first or last. Strike the same note on the piano over and over again. This will give you some idea of the displeasing, jarring effect monotony has on the ear. The dictionary defines "monotonous" as being synonymous with "wearisome." That is putting it mildly. It is maddening. The department-store prince does not disgust the public by playing only the one tune, "Come Buy My Wares!" He gives recitals on a $125,000 organ, and the pleased people naturally slip into a buying mood. How to Conquer Monotony We obviate monotony in dress by replenishing our wardrobes. We avoid monotony in speech by multiplying our powers of speech. We multiply our powers of speech by increasing our tools. The carpenter has special implements with which to construct the several parts of a building. The organist has certain keys and stops which he manipulates to produce his harmonies and effects. In like manner the speaker has certain instruments and tools at his command by which he builds his argument, plays on the feelings, and guides the beliefs of his audience. To give you a conception of these instruments, and practical help in learning to use them, are the purposes of the immediately following chapters. Why did not the Children of Israel whirl through the desert in limousines, and why did not Noah have moving-picture entertainments and talking machines on the Ark? The laws that enable us to operate an automobile, produce moving-pictures, or music on the Victrola, would have worked just as well then as they do today. It was ignorance of law that for ages deprived humanity of our modern conveniences. Many speakers still use ox-cart methods in their speech instead of employing automobile or overland-express methods. They are ignorant of laws that make for efficiency in speaking. Just to the extent that you regard and use the laws that we are about to examine and learn how to use will you have efficiency and force in your speaking; and just to the extent that you disregard them will your speaking be feeble and ineffective. We cannot impress too thoroughly upon you the necessity for a real working mastery of these principles. They are the very foundations of successful speaking. "Get your principles right," said Napoleon, "and the rest is a matter of detail." It is useless to shoe a dead horse, and all the sound principles in Christendom will never make a live speech out of a dead one. So let it be understood that public speaking is not a matter of mastering a few dead rules; the most important law of public speech is the necessity for truth, force, feeling, and life. Forget all else, but not this. When you have mastered the mechanics of speech outlined in the next few chapters you will no longer be troubled with monotony. The complete knowledge of these principles and the ability to apply them will give you great variety in your powers of expression. But they cannot be mastered and applied by thinking or reading about them--you must practise, practise, PRACTISE. If no one else will listen to you, listen to yourself--you must always be your own best critic, and the severest one of all. The technical principles that we lay down in the following chapters are not arbitrary creations of our own. They are all founded on the practices that good speakers and actors adopt--either naturally and unconsciously or under instruction--in getting their effects. It is useless to warn the student that he must be natural. To be natural may be to be monotonous. The little strawberry up in the arctics with a few tiny seeds and an acid tang is a natural berry, but it is not to be compared with the improved variety that we enjoy here. The dwarfed oak on the rocky hillside is natural, but a poor thing compared with the beautiful tree found in the rich, moist bottom lands. Be natural--but improve your natural gifts until you have approached the ideal, for we must strive after idealized nature, in fruit, tree, and speech. Think of any project you want to accomplish: Getting started is probably the most difficult part of the entire process. The same applies to organizing speeches. Many people dread the process of writing and preparing a speech so much that they put it off until they find themselves two days from the actual day of the presentation—and panic sets in. Here is where some of you may have contemplated calling in sick and asking the group you will be addressing to find someone else. However, guilt sets in and somehow you find the courage to get started, and you quickly throw together a speech or presentation. You deliver the speech the next day and manage to get through the event. Let's be honest, how many of you have actually used this "do or die" approach? Many of you, I'm sure. You have heard the expression "Rome wasn't built in a day." Great presentations aren't built in a day, either, unless you are trying to demonstrate how not to prepare a presentation. In most cases it fails and you say to yourself, I will never volunteer to give a speech again The problem with the hasty approach is that you set yourself up for failure and then try to convince yourself that this public speaking stuff is not for you. If you had a method to quickly organize your thoughts, a way to structure your speech, and additional time to practice (practice? you say. What's that?), you would be the hit of the event. Lack of preparation, also known as waiting until the last minute, is one of the biggest contributors to the speech anxiety I discussed in Day 1. Remember from Day 1 that the number one thing you can do to help overcome your speech anxiety is to prepare. My seminar participants often ask me, "When should I start preparing for a presentation?" I always say to them, "The moment they ask you!" Here is an example: Your boss comes up to you and says, "I would like you to prepare [there's that word again] a presentation for the new staff members on Monday and give them an overview of what our group really does—goals, objectives, the whole nine yards. I really want it to be special, and I am counting on you." Several thoughts race through your mind at this time. How can I get someone else to do this? Why couldn't he have asked someone else? Why me? Before you realize it, you open your mouth and the words come blurting out: "No problem, I'd love to." Somehow your mouth and brain did not talk to each other, and you find yourself agreeing! You then proceed to spend the rest of the week worrying about the speech, losing sleep over what you are going to say and how you are going to say it. Before you know it, you realize that tomorrow is the day, and you finally begin to prepare for your presentation. This approach will not work. The first step in creating a great presentation is to gather information. Following are examples of how I and another professional speaker gather information in preparation for presentations. Let's see what the experts have to say Quick Tips to Start Organizing Information About Yourself A good way to start organizing stories about yourself is with your family. Include stories about your parents, your children, your pets, your neighbors. Think back to your childhood and school days. Jot down notes about experiences that have happened to you in your life, good, bad, and unusual; funny, dramatic, expected, and unexpected. The idea is to gather as much material as you can and start to record and organize it into categories. The same approach works well when preparing your actual speech. The key is to collect as much data as possible, whether you use it or not. For example, I keep a little notepad in my car or pocket so I can write down ideas that I might be able to use later. Take a small notepad and pencil when you are exercising. Some of the greatest ideas have come to me while walking on the treadmill or around my neighborhood. Having a spot to write down these ideas the minute you think of them is a plus. If you think you will remember them when you get home, think again. Recording these ideas a few weeks ahead helps you better prepare for the speech. Try to write down how these ideas relate to the audience and your presentation. This proven method alleviates the pressure from having to start from scratch.

Speech Preparation as a Process Genuine speech preparation means looking within yourself. You need to gather facts and arrange these facts in conjunction with your thoughts. It is not enough simply to collect ideas. You must also nurture and reflect on them and decide how to present the ideas in a unique, organized manner. I will go into more detail on the structure of your speech later in the chapter. Following are some tips to get you started preparing for your next speech or presentation. Whether you are talking to a small group or addressing a large auditorium of people, these tips will put you on the path to successful speech giving. • A speech needs time to grow—prepare for weeks. • Sleep on your topic, dream about it, and let your ideas sink into your subconscious. • Ask yourself questions. • Write down your thoughts. • Keep adding new ideas. Once you have determined the purpose (to expand your audience's knowledge of eighteenth-century law) for delivering this speech, state the purpose in a sentence (write it down) and focus your speech around it. Ask yourself, How does this purpose relate to the audience? Write down your answers. Let your purpose drive your speech. A good speech title doesn't hurt, either. Aim not only to inform your listeners, but also to persuade them.

As you prepare each speech, choose a simple structure: • Sequential. Will the material follow chronological order or how the events happened?

Categorical. Will the speech be structured according to the categories? If so, will you talk about the most important category first or last? • Problem and solution. Will your speech be designed to state a dilemma and then offer a device to address the problem? • Contrast and comparison. Will your speech discuss similarities and differences between/among your main points? Outline Regardless of its length, your speech should contain the following main sections: 1. The introduction 2. The body 3. The conclusion Let's take a look at each of these three sections in detail. • The Introduction. The introduction actually consists of three parts: the introductory grabber, the purpose, and the agenda. The introductory grabber is an opening— a pertinent quote or some shocking information or statistics. You can even start with something humorous. The purpose of the speech should focus on the benefits to the listeners. Most listeners want to know "What's in it for me?" The purpose answers that question. The agenda highlights the points that you will cover in your speech. • The Body. This is the meat of your speech or presentation, where you present and discuss the main ideas. The number of points you choose to discuss depends on the length of your speech. Here are some general guidelines on the number of main points you should discuss given a certain length of time.If you remember in my sample speech in Day 1, I briefly discussed my wife, Joan; my son, Michael; and my daughter, Kelly. The level of detail was brief but to the point. I could easily have expanded on any of that information to make a longer speech. The structure would remain the same, but the level of detail would increase. • The Conclusion. Your conclusion serves as a brief review and should leave the listeners thinking about what you said. It is usually divided into three parts: 1. The review. This section reiterates the purpose of the speech and highlights the answers to the audience's question "What's in it for me?" 2. The call to action. During this segment, tell the audience what to do with the information you've presented. 3. The closing grabber. This consists of your closing remarks and should leave listeners with at least one memorable thought. Picking Apart a Speech Let's take my short sample speech example provided in Day 1 and see how to identify the main message, objectives, purpose, central ideas, conclusion, and so on.Here is the list of ten objectives—the body of the speech— that my client presented, along with his main talking points. 1. Oral and written communication skills. Communication skills cover far more than spelling and grammar. Students need to develop the ability to communicate effectively with the entire world. In business communications that may include everything from internal memos to business letters to formal speeches and e-mail. As cyberspace grows and cable systems expand, digital communication provides instant global access. The Internet has truly made this a smaller world, a world in which we must become more diverse in the way we think, reason, and exchange information. 2. Critical thinking, reasoning, and problem-solving skills. "Problem-solving skills" almost seems an ambiguous term. After all, no two problems are identical or require the same solution. Problem solving, then, requires a range of abilities that work in conjunction with one another, such as listening, communicating, critical analysis, research, and creativity. We hear a lot these days about the need for critical thinking skills in the workplace, but we don't hear a lot about how students can acquire these skills. I believe that courses in the humanities, such as literature, philosophy, composition, and history, which require written and verbal analysis, will provide ideal circumstances for our students to develop their analytical abilities. While critical thinking is important, so is creative thinking, or what many refer to as "thinking outside the box." Being able to identify, analyze, and construct a solution to a problem is a skill we all need to succeed. Individuals with imagination and ambition will discover that the greatest source of wealth will be the ideas in their head. 3. Ethical skills. Many of us have difficulty defining the term ethics, yet most education experts agree that we need to nurture a firmer commitment to ethics in students. To survive and prosper in the twenty-first century, students also need self-discipline, which entails an ethical code and the ability to set and assess progress toward their own goals. By introducing students to ethics through specific applications and in relation to specific fields, we can render a more relevant component of civil life that often remains unexamined and unexplored. 4. Use of computers and other technical skills. The use of computers and technology has become an important— indeed, practical—part of today's workforce. Technology will most likely play a vital role in redesigning education systems in the twenty-first century. Commerce on the Internet is driven by computing and telecommunications technology. Experts predict that in 2007 the basic home computer will have 4,000 megabytes of RAM and 300,000 megabytes of storage. The Internet is bringing into every home an astonishing array of learning and commercial opportunities.

5. Teamwork skills. Job success relies on interpersonal, human relations skills and the ability to work as part of a team. Working together is an art that requires practice and expertise. Humanities courses can offer a range of opportunities for students to develop teamwork skills. The workforce of tomorrow will be more diverse than today. Our ability to develop interpersonal skills will continue to play a vital role, even with the surge

in home-based businesses and increased emphasis on technology. Interpersonal skills will divide the workers from the achievers. 6. Adaptability and flexibility skills. In a fast-changing world students need a catalog of skills that are broad and deep enough to enable them to adapt to changing circumstances and to develop attitudes that encourage flexibility. Those students who learn to adapt as the business world changes will continue to succeed. Managing yourself in a world of uncertainty, opportunity, and rapid change will be the greatest challenge in the next ten years. 7. Conflict resolution and negotiation skills. It is essential that all elementary and high school curricula incorporate conflict resolution skills. The curriculum should provide skill-building activities that will give students practice in preventing, defusing, and avoiding conflicts. Students need to learn how to control anger, listen, and work toward a solution with their peers. These skills play a vital role in succeeding in many areas of life, including the workforce. 8. Conduct research, interpret and apply data. Schools need to offer ready access to the world of information through print, electronic, and face-to-face channels. These will provide students with opportunities to test their theories based on what they discover. The United States of America must continue to remain among the world's leaders in every major area of research. A special emphasis must be placed on the development of human resources such as preparing scientists and engineers for a broad range of careers. 9. Multiple languages skills. Communicating effectively in more than one language is important as the marketplace becomes more international. The Internet has already made the world smaller. Speaking another language will be crucial for economic growth and world peace, as well as knowing, appreciating, and working with our global neighbors. 10. Reading and comprehension skills. Along with reading are listening, speaking, writing, and thinking skills. Reading is basic to all other areas of the curriculum. Reading is the foundation upon which all other skills are built. Without the right foundation students will have a more difficult time reaching their potential.

The secret to a great presentation is to tell a story. Think back to when you were a kid and your mother or father read you a bedtime story. Kids love stories, and so do adults. People love speakers who tell stories that apply to their message. These personal stories help drive your message home. To tell your "story" effectively, follow these steps: • Begin at the end of your speech. As Stephen Covey says in his book The 7 Habits of Highly Effective People, "Begin with the end in mind." Think about that main message you want people to understand. Then gather the facts and information you believe are pertinent to your message. Recall personal stories when you were a kid, a teenager, or a young adult that you might use. • Use examples your audience can relate to. For example, if you are talking about the latest advance in cardiac medicine, you may want to share a brief story of a patient who benefited from the technology or therapy. • Practice telling your anecdotes as if you were telling the story for the first time. As you practice, experiment with different phrases and ways of illustrating your story or example. The best approach is to put yourself in the story and pretend you are the main character of the story. Pretend you are acting in a play, and do some role or character playing. Try to take on the personalities and characters in your story. Use actual names or fictitious names to help define the characters in your story. • Practice each of your stories separately and record them. Get a good idea of how long each story takes. This can vary depending on the level of detail you use.

First develop a long version and then a short version of your story. This will come in handy if you need to adjust your speech time. Figure out what kinds of gestures might be used to add some dynamics to your story, such as a change in your voice, how you will move, or whether sitting or standing would be more effective. I will go into storytelling in greater detail in Day 5, where I will discuss body language and voice. Remember, tell them what you are going to tell them. You can't do this until you have figured out what you will be talking about. Tell them—this is where the meat of your speech is—your stories, and tell them what you told them—this is where you do a quick review at the end, telling them what your stories were supposed to tell them, just in case they did not automatically figure it out for themselves.

One of the very last things you do when preparing and organizing your speech is to make adjustments in your timing. To do this effectively, make an audiotape or videotape of your speech and note how long each section of your speech took you to present. To record your speech at this point, set up your video camera or turn on your cassette recorder when you are ready and give your entire speech as if you were doing it for a live audience. It is amazing how many people never even record their presentations and use them as part of their practice. Many people never even practice their speech at all, and they wonder why they have too much speech left over at the end of their time allotment. You will use this same taping technique throughout this book. For the purpose of this chapter, you need only record the start and end times for each section of your speech. Write down the times and keep your notes handy. I recommend the following general time guidelines for each section: • The introduction (10 to 15 percent) • The body (70 to 80 percent) • The conclusion (10 to 15 percent) Let's look at an actual example: Say you are asked to give a speech with a 10-minute time frame. Using the higher percentages just listed, you should allow 15 percent of 10 minutes, or 11⁄2 minutes, for your introduction and 11⁄2 minutes for your conclusion. This leaves only 7 minutes for the actual body of your presentation. If you want a question and answer (Q&A) period at the end of your presentation, you need to allocate additional time for it. Let's say you allow for a 2-minute Q&A session at the end of your presentation. You now have 8 minutes for your presentation. This brings you to your first reality check; with 11⁄2 minutes each for your introduction and conclusion, you now in fact have only 5 minutes for your content (body of speech)—not the 10 minutes you originally assumed. Over my years as a professional speech coach, I have witnessed how most presenters do not use this simple math exercise when preparing their presentations. It is not a surprise to me when they actually run out of time or, worse, run well beyond their allotted time. They may have estimated ten minutes' worth of material, but they did not allow the necessary time for their introduction, conclusion, or Q&A session. Now here is step two. Seeing that you have only five minutes for the actual body of your talk, let's also assume you will be using three stories you developed. The first question to ask yourself is, "Can I tell the three stories in the five minutes?" If not, consider using only two stories or maybe just one. Look at your videotape. Let's say it shows that story one took three minutes, story two took four minutes, and story three took six minutes. That is a total of thirteen minutes! But you have allotted only five minutes. You have a few decisions to make at this point: • If you really want to use all three stories, can you shorten them so their combined total is less than five minutes? Keep in mind you will also need to provide a summary of the main message for each story. Even if that summary is only twenty to thirty seconds, you will need at least one minute for summaries, leaving you really only four minutes. • In this case, I suggest using only two stories, since most stories cannot be told effectively in less than two minutes. You now need to decide on which two stories to tell. I recommend you always include your personal story and present it last. You now have four minutes to use between the two stories. • I suggest you keep the first story very short (only about one to two minutes) and allow yourself the two to three minutes for your personal story. Cutting Story Length Assume that you will use story one and story three, your personal story. You see that initially it took three minutes for story one and five minutes to tell your personal story. You now need to cut each of these stories in half. Here is how you do this. Go back and review the tape of each story and write down the main ideas discussed and the sequence of the ideas used in your original version. Notice the level of detail you used for each idea or section of your story. Decide if you can eliminate any sections or details altogether or determine how you can retell that section of the story in a more concise manner. If you haven't noticed, this is a lot of work! I didn't say it would be easy. Rerecord the story and see how your time has improved. Repeat this process for each story, paying attention to what parts of your stories can be told with less detail. Make mental or written notes during this process because you can use this information later when you are asked to give the same speech but are given more time. The key is not to change the structure of your speech, but to reduce the level of detail. This is why it takes longer to prepare a shorter presentation than a longer one, because you need to constantly refine and rework your story, using fewer words and details but still keeping it intact. Rerecord your entire speech and address the timing again, making additional adjustments as needed. Remember, you will have to work harder at sounding natural if you are modifying personal stories that you are comfortable relaying in detail with no time constraints.

CHAPTER THREE

Relating to Your Audience

You now know the importance of properly preparing your material far enough in advance so you have sufficient time to rehearse and fine-tune your speech. Preparation alone, however, does not guarantee that your speech or presentation will be well received. You must also analyze and relate to your audience. Audience Analysis—It's Your Key to Success Many speakers overlook the need to include any kind of audience analysis as part of their speech preparation. Proper audience analysis makes it possible for you to give the most effective, meaningful, and memorable speech to your audience. Most professional speakers send their clients, the person or company/organization representative who hired the speaker, a multipage questionnaire in order to gather information about the client and the speaking engagement. Having this information allows you to customize your presentation or speech for maximum impact. Using the word AUDIENCE as an acronym, I have provided two sets of audience analysis questions, as well as ideas and tips on how you can use the results to customize your speeches. Let's assume that you have been asked by IDEA (the International Dance and Exercise Alliance) to speak at an upcoming sports and fitness conference in New York. What do you need to do to get started? There are two phases of audience analysis: the preprogram survey and the customized program survey. Both address the following areas that spell out the acronym AUDIENCE. • Analysis. Who is your audience? How many will be attending your presentation? • Understanding. What is their knowledge about the subject on which you plan to speak? • Demographics. Where are they from? What is their age, sex, and educational background? • Interest. Why will they be attending the conference/convention/event? Who asked them to attend, or will they be participating of their own accord? • Environment. Where will you stand? Will everyone be able to see and hear you? • Needs. What are their needs with respect to the speech topic? •

Customized. What do you need to address in your speech (examples, issues, and so on) to meet the audience's needs? • Expectations. What do you think they expect to learn or hear from you?

To help you develop a better idea of the type of information you need for audience analysis, here's a detailed list of information you need to gather about your audience. Both surveys can be done by mail, by fax, or over the telephone. Preprogram Survey The preprogram survey provides general information about your audience. The survey gives you a start on your audience analysis and may even help you pick your topic or angle for your speech. The survey is designed to help you prepare the best presentation possible for your audience. Before doing my survey, I usually call the client or client's representative to get to know him or her better and get a feel for what the client's needs are. Begin working on your preprogram when you are asked to give a presentation; don't wait until the last minute. Here is the preprogram survey: 1. What is the audience's knowledge and level of vocabulary on the topic? Does the audience have expert knowledge, some knowledge, or very little knowledge? 2. How large is the audience? What does the room look like where I will be speaking? What are the options for using visual aids? 3. Is this event focused around a special project or event? 4. Will there be other speakers before or after me on the program? 5. Will there be drinking or eating before my presentation?

6. Have other speakers addressed this audience on a similar topic? 7. If so, what has the audience responded to most positively? 8. What has the audience responded to least positively? 9. What kind of data, information, and support will persuade your audience? 10. What is your group's major needs, problems, and concerns? 11. How much time will I have to speak? 12. What is their relationship to me as a speaker? 13. What is their level of education? 14. What is the ratio of men to women? 15. What are their ages or range of ages? 16. What is their ethnic background? 17. What is their religion? 18. What is their occupation or profession? The responses from your survey give you a better idea what to expect from your audience and what challenges you have planning your presentation. I rely on the results of the preprogram survey to give me the opportunity to add or modify materials to my program.

The customized survey is more in-depth, asking specific questions about the members of the organization and letting you know any information to avoid speaking about. Begin your customized program survey when you have chosen your topic and completed the nitty-gritty of your outline. At this point, it's appropriate to recontact your liaison for the presentation about this survey. Some of the customized program survey questions are similar to the preprogram survey; that's intentional. 1. What is the theme of the meeting? 2. What are the top challenges or problems faced by members of the group? 3. What, approximately, are the characteristics of your average member? Age: —— Annual Income: —— Educational Background: —— Sex: —— Occupation: —— 4. Will there be any other special guests? 5. How many people will be in the audience? 6. Why is this group attending this meeting? 7. How will they be notified? 8. What is the audience's overall opinion regarding this subject? (favorable, hostile, etc.) 9. What three facts should I know about the group before addressing them? 10. What speakers have you used in the past, and what did they discuss? 11. What speakers/ programs have been most enthusiastically received? 12. Please list the names and positions of three people in your organization who are well known and well liked within the group who will be present during my speech. 13. Whom can I call on or joke with if the need arises?14. What are the three most significant events that have occurred in your industry, or within your group, during the past year? 15. Please share any local "color" you can think of that relates to the location where my speech will be held. 16. Specifically, what are you trying to accomplish at this meeting? 17. What are your specific objectives for my part of the meeting? 18. Are there any issues/topics in particular that you think I should discuss during the program? 19. Are there any issues/topics in particular that you think I should avoid during the program? 20. Do you have any suggestions to help me make this presentation the best your audience has ever heard? Again, the responses help you tailor your presentation to the audience. It is up to you to develop your own list of specific questions to use for preparing your program. Take the lists I have just provided and adapt them to your own needs. Remember, the more you know about your audience the better.

When an audience is invited to hear a speaker, they seldom walk into that presentation hoping the speaker is boring or fails miserably. When was the last time you went to a seminar and said to yourself, I hope I get nothing out of this seminar and I won't mind if I wasted my money? What you are more likely to say is, I hope this seminar provides some valuable information, insight, specific tools, or techniques I can start using today to help me with my job. An audience wants to feel that your speech, seminar, or presentation has direct relevance to them. People may be looking for answers to help them with problems they have at home or at work. An audience wants to feel that you care about and understand them. This is where your audience analysis comes in handy. The more in-depth your audience analysis questions, the more prepared you are to understand the psychology of your audience, their needs, and their desires. Knowing this specific information prepares you with the information you need to address these needs during your presentation and have the audience say on your evaluation sheet, "This presenter really understood my problems and was right on the money!" The key to being a successful public speaker is to properly know your audience before you speak to them.

Report talk is delivering your speech in a monotone, flat voice. Often you sound as if you are just reading your speech without any effort to engage your audience. Rapport talk, on the other hand, is delivering your speech in a conversational, lively style. Building rapport with your audience is extremely critical for gaining acceptance. Before I provide you with tips for building a rapport with your audience, I want you first and foremost to realize that you must respect your audience. Treat your audience the way they would expect to be treated by their family, friends, and co-workers by being courteous and attentive to their questions and requests. • Greet your audience. One of the most effective strategies I use at my seminars is to greet people as they enter the room. This demonstrates that you are accessible and approachable. I make sure I arrive early enough so everything is set up properly. By doing this, I'm able to greet people and help establish an immediate connection. • Begin on time. If you are scheduled to start at nine A.M. and 90 percent of the seminar attendees are present, then start on time. Many speakers believe they should wait a few minutes to allow everyone to get there, but don't. You show respect to those people who went the extra mile to arrive early and on time. Why should they have to wait? • Recognize people by name. If possible, I try to remember the audience names by encouraging them to wear their name tag. This lets you call on people by their names and makes the environment more personal. • Establish eye contact. They say the eyes are the mirror to the soul, and having good eye contact with your audience demonstrates your true interest in them. This is especially true if you are engaged in a one-on-one conversation with an audience member. Make eye contact with as many people in your audience as possible. Be careful not to talk to the same few people in the front row. • Pay attention. When people ask you a question or offer comments during the seminar, show them respect by paying close attention to what they have to say. Repeat the question for the entire audience. For example, you could say, "Mary from . . . just asked me a question about . . ." This shows respect to Mary, and you use her name .

Schedule breaks. Giving the audience a break allows them to attend to personal business such as calling in to their office, and it gives them a rest, but it also allows you time to mingle with people in the audience and get to know them better. Through impromptu conversations, you can gauge the audience's reactions to the program up to that point. Tell people what time to be back from breaks. • Reward people for suggestions. I have delivered many seminars where someone in the audience really participates and makes a valuable or thought-provoking suggestion that in some way has enriched the seminar. As an incentive to encourage people to participate, I give volunteers a small gift that is related to speaking or presentation skills and something they can use in their own presentations, such as one of my videotapes or audiotapes or colored markers. • Make yourself available. I make it a policy to be accessible by phone, fax, and e-mail to people who attend my seminars. This gives them the opportunity to ask more questions and shows that I really care about their learning.

CHAPTER FOUR

EMPHASIS AND SUBORDINATION

The gun that scatters too much does not bag the birds. The same principle applies to speech. The speaker that fires his force and emphasis at random into a sentence will not get results. Not every word is of special importance--therefore only certain words demand emphasis. You say MassaCHUsetts and MinneAPolis, you do not emphasize each syllable alike, but hit the accented syllable with force and hurry over the unimportant ones. Now why do you not apply this principle in speaking a sentence? To some extent you do, in ordinary speech; but do you in public discourse? It is there that monotony caused by lack of emphasis is so painfully apparent. So far as emphasis is concerned, you may consider the average sentence as just one big word, with the important word as the accented syllable. Note the following: "Destiny is not a matter of chance. It is a matter of choice." You might as well say MASS-A-CHU-SETTS, emphasizing every syllable equally, as to lay equal stress on each word in the foregoing sentences. Speak it aloud and see. Of course you will want to emphasize destiny, for it is the principal idea in your declaration, and you will put some emphasis on not, else your hearers may think you are affirming that destiny is a matter of chance. By all means you must emphasize chance, for it is one of the two big ideas in the statement. Another reason why chance takes emphasis is that it is contrasted with choice in the next sentence. Obviously, the author has contrasted these ideas purposely, so that they might be more emphatic, and here we see that contrast is one of the very first devices to gain emphasis. As a public speaker you can assist this emphasis of contrast with your voice. If you say, "My horse is not black," what color immediately comes into mind? White, naturally, for that is the opposite of black. If you wish to bring out the thought that destiny is a matter of choice, you can do so more effectively by first saying that "DESTINY is NOT a matter of CHANCE." Is not the color of the horse impressed upon us more emphatically when you say, "My horse is NOT BLACK. He is WHITE" than it would be by hearing you assert merely that your horse is white? In the second sentence of the statement there is only one important word--choice. It is the one word that positively defines the quality of the subject being discussed, and the author of those lines desired to bring it out emphatically, as he has shown by contrasting it with another idea. These lines, then, would read like this: "DESTINY is NOT a matter of CHANCE. It is a matter of CHOICE." Now read this over, striking the words in capitals with a great deal of force. In almost every sentence there are a few MOUNTAIN PEAK WORDS that represent the big, important ideas. When you pick up the evening paper you can tell at a glance which are the important news articles. Thanks to the editor, he does not tell about a "hold up" in Hong Kong in the same sized type as he uses to report the death of five firemen in your home city. Size of type is his device to show emphasis in bold relief. He brings out sometimes even in red headlines the striking news of the day. It would be a boon to speech-making if speakers would conserve the attention of their audiences in the same way and emphasize only the words representing the important ideas. The average speaker will deliver the foregoing line on destiny with about the same amount of emphasis on each word. Instead of saying, "It is a matter of CHOICE," he will deliver it, "It is a matter of choice," or "IT IS A MATTER OF CHOICE"--both equally bad. Charles Dana, the famous editor of The New York Sun, told one of his reporters that if he went up the street and saw a dog bite a man, to pay no attention to it. The Sun could not afford to waste the time and attention of its readers on such unimportant happenings. "But," said Mr. Dana, "if you see a man bite a dog, hurry back to the office and write the story." Of course that is news; that is unusual. Now the speaker who says "IT IS A MATTER OF CHOICE" is putting too much emphasis upon things that are of no more importance to metropolitan readers than a dog bite, and when he fails to emphasize "choice" he is like the reporter who "passes up" the man's biting a dog. The ideal speaker makes his big words stand out like mountain peaks; his unimportant words are submerged like stream-beds. His big thoughts stand like huge oaks; his ideas of no especial value are merely like the grass around the tree. From all this we may deduce this important principle: EMPHASIS is a matter of CONTRAST and COMPARISON. Recently the New York American featured an editorial by Arthur Brisbane. Note the following, printed in the same type as given here.

=We do not know what the President THOUGHT when he got that message, or what the elephant thinks when he sees the mouse, but we do know what the President DID.= The words THOUGHT and DID immediately catch the reader's attention because they are different from the others, not especially because they are larger. If all the rest of the words in this sentence were made ten times as large as they are, and DID and THOUGHT were kept at their present size, they would still be emphatic, because different. Take the following from Robert Chambers' novel, "The Business of Life." The words you, had, would, are all emphatic, because they have been made different. He looked at her in angry astonishment. "Well, what do you call it if it isn't cowardice--to slink off and marry a defenseless girl like that!" "Did you expect me to give you a chance to destroy me and poison Jacqueline's mind? If I had been guilty of the thing with which you charge me, what I have done would have been cowardly. Otherwise, it is justified." A Fifth Avenue bus would attract attention up at Minisink Ford, New York, while one of the ox teams that frequently pass there would attract attention on Fifth Avenue. To make a word emphatic, deliver it differently from the manner in which the words surrounding it are delivered. If you have been talking loudly, utter the emphatic word in a concentrated whisper--and you have intense emphasis. If you have been going fast, go very slow on the emphatic word. If you have been talking on a low pitch, jump to a high one on the emphatic word. If you have been talking on a high pitch, take a low one on your emphatic ideas. Read the chapters on "Inflection," "Feeling," "Pause," "Change of Pitch," "Change of Tempo." Each of these will explain in detail how to get emphasis through the use of a certain principle. we are considering only one form of emphasis: that of applying force to the important word and subordinating the unimportant words. Do not forget: this is one of the main methods that you must continually employ in getting your effects. Let us not confound loudness with emphasis. To yell is not a sign of earnestness, intelligence, or feeling. The kind of force that we want applied to the emphatic word is not entirely physical. True, the emphatic word may be spoken more loudly, or it may be spoken more softly, but the real quality desired is intensity, earnestness. It must come from within, outward. Last night a speaker said: "The curse of this country is not a lack of education. It's politics." He emphasized curse, lack, education, politics. The other words were hurried over and thus given no comparative importance at all. The word politics was flamed out with great feeling as he slapped his hands together indignantly. His emphasis was both correct and powerful.

He concentrated all our attention on the words that meant something, instead of holding it up on such words as of this, a, of, It's. What would you think of a guide who agreed to show New York to a stranger and then took up his time by visiting Chinese laundries and boot-blacking "parlors" on the side streets? There is only one excuse for a speaker's asking the attention of his audience: He must have either truth or entertainment for them. If he wearies their attention with trifles they will have neither vivacity nor desire left when he reaches words of Wall-Street and skyscraper importance. You do not dwell on these small words in your everyday conversation, because you are not a conversational bore. Apply the correct method of everyday speech to the platform. As we have noted elsewhere, public speaking is very much like conversation enlarged. Sometimes, for big emphasis, it is advisable to lay stress on every single syllable in a word, as absolutely in the following sentence: I ab-so-lute-ly refuse to grant your demand. Now and then this principle should be applied to an emphatic sentence by stressing each word. It is a good device for exciting special attention, and it furnishes a pleasing variety. Patrick Henry's notable climax could be delivered in that manner very effectively: "Give--me--liberty--or--give--me--death." The italicized part of the following might also be delivered with this every-word emphasis. Of course, there are many ways of delivering it; this is only one of several good interpretations that might be chosen.

CHAPTER FIVE

Remembering What You Have to Say

Remembering speech and presentation material can be very intimidating, even for the most seasoned professional. But don't worry, there are many methods you can use to help you remember material—all of them will help build your confidence in public speaking. Techniques for Remembering Speech Material The four most common methods of remembering speech and presentation material are the following: 1. Memorizing 2. Reading from complete text 3. Using notes 4. Using visual aids Let's take a look at each of these in more detail, including the pros and cons. You will notice that some of the tips apply to all the methods; that's okay, it only emphasizes their importance. Memorizing Perhaps the most difficult of the four methods, memorizing is the technique many novice speakers start off with, because they are under the impression that this is how all speeches are prepared and delivered. I actually do not recommend memorizing your speech: Although the outcome can be very effective, memorizing a speech word for word and then delivering it requires a lot of preparation and practice. First you must write or type out the speech. Since most people do not write the way they speak, this creates an immediate problem. For example, the use of gestures and proper voice inflection in conjunction with a memorized speech tends to be very flat and unengaging. Even if you are successful in using gestures and a lively tone of voice, it's entirely possible that you will forget portions of your speech. Listening to thousands of speeches over my career, I have watched even the most polished speakers forget their words halfway through. With memorizing, mental blocks are inevitable, and it is not a question of "Will you forget?" but "when you will forget?" Can you memorize a speech? Yes. Should you memorize a speech? I don't recommend it. Speakers who rely strictly on memorization are setting themselves up for failure. Another risk factor with memorized speeches is that the spontaneity is gone—you sound stilted. What tends to happen is that the delivery is too rapid (usually owing to nerves). Your concentration is on getting the words out, not the ideas, and you tend to come across as too formal, like a written essay. Worst of all, if your mind goes blank and you make a mistake, the flow of your speech is interrupted. You get flus tered, your confidence is shot, and in most cases it's just not appropriate to start over. Reading from Complete Text Most people dislike listening to someone read a speech or presentation, even if the speaker makes a concerted effort to maintain eye contact with the audience. Your audience is just likely to end up saying, "If all he was going to do was read his speech, I could have read it myself." I'm sure each of you has experienced the monotone drone of a read speech while attending a conference. Following are the reasons I believe people read speeches poorly: • The speaker loses normal voice inflection because he loses touch with the ideas behind the words. Listen for pauses. Natural speech is filled with pauses; unnatural speech is not. • The text being read is usually not written in the manner and style of spoken language. Too often speakers write their speeches in "business language" that is often very difficult to read, much less listen to. • The speaker achieves little or no eye contact. Any eye contact is with the manuscript and not with the audience. To maintain eye contact with the audience and read text effectively takes a lot of practice. You have to take in several lines at a time and keep your place. You are very likely to find yourself losing your place every time you look up to speak to the audience. Don't get me wrong, there are times when speeches must be read. For example, it is often necessary to read policy statements or company announcements. To avoid mistakes when some element of a speech must be communicated word for 71 Remembering What You Have to Say word, the speaker reads directly from written text. There are also occasions when a speech must be timed down to the second, as in a debate. In my opinion, reading a speech well is actually more difficult than speaking extemporaneously. Although people hear all the time that they should not read their speech, most feel this is the only way they can actually give one. For those of you who feel compelled to read your speech, I'll help you at least sound better when you do. If reading is absolutely necessary, here are some suggestions to make your reading sound more professional. • Pay attention to your voice inflection. To sound natural you need to rehearse often, checking yourself for pauses. Ask yourself if your written words sound the way you would speak them. Tape yourself and listen to your own voice. Note where changes need to be made with your voice inflection. Try not to overinflect your voice or it will become distracting to your audience. • Say the words out loud. As you're practicing your speech, read it out loud several times so you can hear your tone and voice inflection. The more you practice reading, the more comfortable and familiar with the words you become. Using this approach makes it easier to read your speech and for the audience to listen to it. • Annotate your text. Give yourself cues for emphasis in the margin of your text. For example, numbers are the easiest target words to say slowly and with emphasis. You want to emphasize each syllable of any number word. For example, if you have the word fifty in your speech, and it appears as 50, make a note in the margin, so you say "fif-ty" when you get to it. • Use gestures. Many speakers are so busy making sure they read the text correctly, they fail to communicate effectively with their body. One strategy is to doublespace your typed text. This leaves room for you to jot down notes and cues about which words to emphasize and gestures to accompany certain sentences, points, or key messages. You need to practice the annotated text of the speech so you can correctly read it and identify cues for your gestures so they come across naturally. This takes practice. Professionals do this very effectively to the point where you almost don't know they are reading. Again, don't overgesture or it can draw your audience away from listening to your message. • Videotape yourself. I still videotape my speeches and presentations, especially those I deliver for the first time. I recommend you sit down with a pen and paper in your hand and take notes as you watch your video. Watch the video several times, each time taking notes on different things you see. Here is the process I use to review my videotapes: • Review 1. Watch the entire tape (alone) without being too critical. Watch the tape as an audience might for the first time. • Review 2. Darken the picture or turn your back to the television so you cannot see yourself but you can hear your voice. Record on your notepad things you liked and disliked about your voice; for example, listen to how you phrase your words and the inflection in your voice. • Review 3. Turn down the sound and just watch yourself. Watch how you use your hands, your facial expressions, or any nervous habits or distracting mannerisms. Again, record the things you want to change, improve, or eliminate. At the same time, note any gestures you feel work well and look natural. • Review 4. Watch the tape again with the volume turned up and take more notes. See if there are any areas you missed during earlier reviews. • Review 5.

Have someone else watch the tape who will be honest and objective, such as your spouse, child, friend, and so on. As they watch the video, look at their reactions to your speech and then ask them, after the tape is done, to tell you what they liked and disliked. Having watched your own video four times prior, you are prepared to deal with any feedback, even negative. This review process is probably the single best technique you can use to help you learn, improve, and modify how you deliver a speech or presentation .

Keep it brief. Don't write out whole paragraphs of text. Put only a few key words or phrases on each card, just enough to jog your memory. Also put only one or two ideas on each card, and print large and neatly so your notes are easy to read. • Remember to number your note cards! Just in case you drop them. • Include quotes, statistics, and lists. Don't include whole paragraphs of text. • Leave your notes on the lectern or table as you're speaking and move away occasionally. Don't be afraid to move away from your notes and get out of your comfort zone. Too many speakers use the lectern to hide behind, and this restricts the use of your body. If the notes are in your hand, you won't gesture as often. • Practice using your note cards. Practice helps you analyze your note cards. For example, if you find yourself reading from your note cards too much, reduce the amount of written text on your cards. • Use pictures and maps. You don't have to use just words on your note cards. Pictures and maps help you visualize the key points of your speech. In some cases it's best to draw a sketch or diagram on your note cards. Sometimes a simple drawing is all you need to jog your memory. Also use mental pictures to tell a story in your mind. This takes creativity, but it's worth the effort. For example, picture in your mind the events as they unfold. As you relive the story, whether it's true or fictional, it's easier to visualize your speech as a story rather than a group of words written in a certain order.

Simple visual aids effectively serve as headings or subheadings on your topic and allow your audience to visually see what you are discussing. Create meaningful headings, and practice using only these headings as your cues. This takes time to master, but practicing helps you internalize your speech. For example, one visual aid might read, "How to structure a presentation." Then you can speak extemporaneously from what you know. If you have properly prepared your speech, you can speak in a conversational manner. When I give a presentation I use slides. Here is an example of a slide I use when giving a seminar entitled "How to Overcome Speaking Anxiety in Meetings and Presentations." • Symptoms of Speaking

Anxiety —Anxiety. —Sweaty palms. —Nervousness. • Mental Techniques to Reduce Speaking Anxiety —Prepare and rehearse. —Use positive self-talk. —Be natural, but enthusiastic. • Physical Techniques to Reduce Speaking Anxiety —Take a brisk walk before you speak. —Use deep breathing exercises. —Don't sit with your legs crossed. Choosing the right visual aid for your presentation is as important as its design. Following are tips to consider when using visual aids and notes.Use the KISS method. This is an acronym for "Keep it short and simple." Use no more than one idea per visual aid. Use no more than six or seven lines per visual aid and no more than six or seven words per line. • Use descriptive titles. The title of each visual aid should be a simple summary of what is on the visual aid. A clear title helps grab the attention of the audience and helps you and the audience remember your main message for that particular visual aid. • Use the same design for each of your visuals. Use the same color, text size, and font type. The idea is to be visually and stylistically consistent. • Make copies of your handouts. Make sure you bring enough for everyone, and always have extras. I recommend keeping a copy of your handouts for two reasons. First, you have a copy to refer to during your presentation. Also, if you are using an overhead projector and it breaks or the bulb burns out and you don't have a replacement, you can refer to your handouts without stopping the flow of your speech. In addition, I keep an original copy of my handouts, one without notations written on them, in case I need to make any last minute copies for workshop participants. • Proofread your visual aids. Proofread for typos and grammatical errors. Then proof again. Then have someone else proofread them. It is amazing how you can review your own visual aids and skip right over the same misspelled word each time. Having others proofread your slides helps you find other mistakes. Don't assume that the spell checker on your word processor will catch all the errors. For example, if you type "cat" when you meant "chat," your spell checker won't catch that error since "cat" is a word.Keep in mind, your visual aids are not limited to words. They can also contain diagrams, drawings, pictures, or even objects. Regardless of the method you choose for remembering material, nothing helps you more than proper planning, preparation, and practice. Positive Performance: The Most Creative Ideas for Presenting Material As you think about developing presentation material, consider the different ways you've seen presentations delivered. For example, if a presenter pulls out a one-inch-high stack of overhead transparencies, you're likely to say to yourself, This is going to be boring. No one said you couldn't be entertaining while giving a speech or presentation. Your audience needs to be an intricate part of your presentation. Give them something to do during your presentation other than just listen. Be creative. Don't restrict yourself to using only overhead transparencies or slides. Try new things. The Northwestern School of Speech reports that the attention span of an audience is approximately nine seconds. The attention is the highest at the beginning and at the end of the presentation. What this means is that you have a free ride during the first few minutes; however, if you blow the first few minutes, you've lost them for the remaining time. Remember, the audience is always checking you out and asking themselves, Is this going to be worth listening to? or I wish I'd sat in the back near the door so I could sneak out. The solution? Spice up your presentation every six to eight minutes. Add elements to keep it alive, exciting, and interesting. Here are ways to make your presentation come alive.Use humor. In the next section I provide some Web sites that I recommend as resources for polishing speaking skills; note the last one, which deals with humor. Also, trust your instincts and free yourself up to use your own natural sense of humor in appropriate places. • Use information and quotes from newspaper and magazine articles. Find articles that relate to your topic—a human interest story, research results, or an article about the latest industry issue or trend—and incorporate them into your presentation. • Incorporate questions during your presentation. Asking open-ended questions encourages your audience to think. I phrase most of my questions with the five w's: who, what, when, where, and why. Here are two example questions I've asked many times in my seminars: "How many of you think speaking to a large group of people is more difficult than speaking to a small, intimate group?" and "What kinds of symptoms have you experienced when you're nervous about speaking to a group?" These questions can be planned ahead and asked of the group or directed to an individual. • Use analogies. Include any of your "war stories" as part of your presentation. People love hearing stories, but make sure the stories illustrate a point and are not there just to fill the time slot. For example, when I gave my motivational speech to the group at the Mt. Snow ski resort in New England (see Day 3), I compared the challenges of preparing a presentation to the challenges of skiing down a mountain, emphasizing how sometimes you fall, but you force yourself to get back up and try again.

The location where you deliver your speech can enhance or interfere with the effectiveness of your presentation. It is very important to find out what the facilities look like before you speak. It is always best, if possible, to visit in advance the location and room where you will be speaking. If you can't visit beforehand, find out the room layout from the meeting planner, coordinator, or hotel staff. When I make arrangements for my public seminars, I always contact the meeting planner, person in charge of the seminar, or hotel staff and send a sketch of how I want the room laid out. For example, the sketch shows how I want the tables set up (such as classroom style or dinner style) and where I'll be addressing the audience. Here are some points you may want to address with the meeting planner or convention hall or hotel staff: 1. Room location 2. Room size 3. Room layout 4. Chair and table arrangements 5. Door and window locations 6. Lighting 10 Days to More Confident Public Speaking 84 7. Signage: directing the participants to the room location 8. Hotel background music 9. Room temperature controls 10. Other functions taking place in the hotel or convention center during your seminar (find out what's going on in the room next door) 11. Food arrangements 12. Audiovisual requirements 13. Phone lines 14. Storage and security for seminar equipment Let's take a moment to look more closely at each of these factors for creating a professional speaking environment. Room Location Quite often you won't have much control over the room location unless you're presenting in your own company. If possible, visit the conference rooms available to you and decide which room is appropriate for your presentation. • As I said, prepare a diagram of how you want the room set up and mail or fax a copy of it to the corporation or facility where you'll be speaking. • Call the staff member in charge of the seminar and discuss your needs; see if you can make an on-site visit. • Check parking and fees involved, if applicable. Inform attendees ahead of time, by including a note or flyer in preconference mailings. • Send attendees the name and address of the hotel or conference center and the room name or number in which the presentation is being given.

Send attendees a detailed map showing the exact location and directions. Room Size The size of the room you will need depends on the number of people attending your seminar or meeting. Obviously the room size and setup is different for ten people than for several hundred. The room size should provide adequate space for you, your visual aids, your equipment, and your participants. There is nothing worse than being crammed into a room the size of a closet. At the same time, you don't want to feel you are in an auditorium unless you need the larger room to accommodate your group. Here are some more tips. • Arrive early. I like to arrive at least two hours before a speaking engagement. When I travel, I ask to see the room the evening before, if possible. This allows me to make any last minute adjustments with my presentation. • If I am one of many speakers on a program or a multiday conference, I arrive early and sit in the room I will be speaking in to get a feel for it. Room Layout The layout of the room has a tremendous effect on the success of your meeting or seminar. Many hotel staff are not aware of the preferred room layout style required by speakers. A majority of hotels set the rooms in one of two ways: 1. Auditorium or theater style 2. Dinner style 10 Days to More Confident Public Speaking 86 On the following pages I give setup preferences I use at my speaking engagements and a pro and con for each one. The four common room setups are 1. classroom style; 2. U-shaped workshop style; 3. theater style or lecture style; 4. dinner style.

Chair and Table Arrangements • Arrange the chairs in advance with as few rows as possible. Do not have more tables and chairs set up than you need. Most people tend to sit in the back rows of the room and avoid the front row at all costs because they fear being picked on during the presentation to answer a question or participate in a demonstration. • Some speakers put out fewer chairs than they need and leave extras stacked in the back of the room, creating the impression of a full seminar or workshop. • Tape Reserved signs on the back few rows of chairs. This forces the attendees to sit closer to the front. • Provide tables if possible. This gives people a more comfortable place to write. • Don't cram too many chairs behind seminar tables. Most hotel tables seat three people comfortably, but I 91 Remembering What You Have to Say Door prefer to sit only two people per table. This accomplishes two things: first, it gives my seminar participants more room; and second, it forces you to use more tables, creating a fuller seminar room. • Provide soft, comfortable chairs if you are giving an allday or multiday program. • Leave plenty of room between tables and chairs to allow people to move freely around the room. This is especially important if you are providing refreshments during the seminar. Door and Window Locations Arrange the chairs and tables so the doors are at the back of the room, allowing people to arrive and sit down quickly without interrupting you. • Serve refreshments near the back of the room, where most people congregate during breaks and can easily come and go. • Set up a table with your speaking products (if you have them) in the back. For example, I bring copies of my books, videotapes, and audiotapes for participants. In addition, I bring my brochures, product catalogs, and promotional materials to my speaking engagements. If possible, I set up a table in a location where participants enter and exit the room. This encourages them to stop and peruse what I have to offer. Windows are an important part of the room layout. Obviously you have no control of the window location. However, if you believe the windows are a distraction:

See if a room without windows is available; if not, close the curtains or blinds. Lighting Proper lighting plays a key role in your presentation. If the lights are too dim, it could put the participants to sleep. If the lights are too bright, it could bother their eyes and make it hard to see visual aids, especially overhead transparencies and slides. • Check lighting prior to your meeting or seminar. • Ask yourself if it's bright enough for everyone to see. • Make sure you know where the light controls are located and how to use them. For example, if you're using an overhead projector or slide carousel, you'll need to adjust the lights. • Label the switches to remind you what part of the room each controls, such as overhead, back, or front. • Never put the room in complete darkness. • If the room has lamps, turn them off so your audience won't be distracted. It may not be necessary to turn off every lamp. Do what you believe will make the room comfortable for your presentation and audience. • See if it's possible to use a spotlight, or bring in additional lighting if the room is too dark for your liking. Signage If your attendees can't find you or get lost finding you throughout the hotel conference area or convention hall, 93 Remembering What You Have to Say they'll be in a foul mood even before you start your presentation. • Place several signs clearly indicating the room location. This helps if the room is located in a separate wing of the building. • Ask the front desk or welcoming table staff to give attendees directions to the meeting location. Hotel Background Music Music can be distracting during a presentation unless it's part of your program. If you find the room has music: • Find out how to turn it off. Some hotels do not have individual room controls, and you don't want to compete with the music, so ask at the front desk or speak to the person in charge. Some rooms have controls where you can turn off the music yourself. • Use either royalty-free music where you don't have to pay royalties (a fee) to the producer or musical artist, or use music you received permission to play. Several companies on the Internet offer royalty-free music. Occasionally I use lively music when the guests first arrive. I play softer, more soothing music during the breaks. However, the music I choose isn't tied in to my presentation. Room Temperature Controls It's important that the room be comfortable for you and your attendees. • Find out from the hotel or convention hall how to control the room temperature. Many hotel rooms or 10 Days to More Confident Public Speaking 94 convention halls have thermostats, but many times these have a Plexiglas cover and are locked. • Ask if the lock can be removed during your seminar. • Get a name and number to reach the hotel personnel or convention hall manager if you are not permitted to control the temperature. Other Functions at the Same Location Giving a speech is difficult enough. The last thing you need to worry about is the class reunion with a disc jockey next door. • Find out if any other functions are happening simultaneously with your seminar (such as a wedding). • If this is the case, ask if you can move your function to another room. If this happens at the last minute, ask for the hotel staff's help in preparing appropriate signage to direct attendees to the new room. This scenario has occurred only a few times in my professional speaking career. For example, if I learn a wedding is next door and I can't change my room, I try to get a time frame from someone involved in the wedding reception. I can find out when the "loud" portions of the wedding are occurring, such as introducing the bridal party and cutting the cake, so I'm not competing with the noise. As your presentation skills improve, you may find yourself being asked to give a speech or say a few words about an associate, friend, or family member at a special event or occasion. Often you don't have time to prepare. Following are tips I used to give a spontaneous speech following a dance recital at which my daughter received her first dance trophy. I remember when Kelly first began to dance and perform; she was only two. During her years as a dancer, we would stop for ice cream after each recital to celebrate what a great job she did. At most recitals, those dancers who have performed for five or more years are usually presented with a trophy to acknowledge their accomplishment. When Kelly received her first trophy we again went out for ice cream and invited the group who came to see Kelly to join us. On this occasion I gave a short speech about what a great job she did and how proud she made her family. This short speech had only a few main points: • Thank the people who attended the recital for showing Kelly their support. • Congratulate Kelly for doing a great job. • Acknowledge the fact that she received an award. I then closed by saying, "Let's dig in." So the next time you have an opportunity to give a speech to celebrate an achievement, you can at least do the following even if you don't have time to prepare: • Decide how you want to begin the speech. In my example, I thanked people for coming. 10 Days to More Confident Public Speaking 98 • Acknowledge the person receiving the achievement. Make sure you mention the name of the achievement or award and what it means. • Include a personal story about the person being honored—keep it fun and upbeat.

CHAPTER SIX

Body Language and Voice

Research has demonstrated that over half of all human communication takes place on the nonverbal level. When you speak before a group, your listeners base their judgment of you and your message on what they see as well as on what they hear. Your body is an effective tool for adding emphasis and clarity to your words. It's also your most powerful instrument for convincing an audience of your sincerity, earnestness, and enthusiasm. However, if your physical actions don't agree with your verbal message, your body can defeat your words. Remember the following credo: Effective speech delivery involves the whole person. Positive Performance: Letting Your Body Mirror Your Message You can learn to use your entire body as an instrument of speech. As the speaker, you are the most important visual aid for your audience. Here are reasons you are important: 1. You don't have to darken the room to be seen. 2. You don't burn out. 3. You don't jam up. 4. You don't break. 5. You aren't one-dimensional. 6. You don't need a technician to operate you. Developing your body language starts with examining the nonverbal messages a speaker gives, including these: • Proper speaking posture • Gestures • Body movement/walking patterns • Facial expressions • Eye contact • Your overall appearance When you present a speech, your listeners use their eyes and ears, as well as their own people instincts, to determine whether you • are sincere. • welcome the opportunity to speak to the audience. • truly believe what you are saying. • are interested in the audience and care about them. • are confident and in control. Here's another important credo: Physical actions speak louder than words. Consider the following example. Shuffling his notes, a man staggers to the podium. He clears his throat, grabs the lectern tightly, and plunges into his speech by saying, "It's a 101 Say It with Style great pleasure to be here today. I have a message of extreme importance to you." The effect of these opening remarks was anything but positive. Although his words expressed pleasure in addressing his audience, he transmitted a clearly contradictory nonverbal message: "I'm in terrible discomfort. I don't actually want to be anywhere near here." This man's visual messages may have been generated by nervousness and inexperience or actual physical discomfort and were transmitted unconsciously. His nonverbal communication branded him as insincere, indifferent, and incompetent, even though he was none of these things. When you speak, your audience tends to mirror your attitudes as they perceive them through their senses. For example, if you're unenthusiastic, your audience will feel that way, too. If you appear nervous, your audience will probably be nervous. If you fidget, they will perceive a lack of self-control in you and will be likely to doubt your message. It is vital, therefore, that your body faithfully portray your true feelings and intent, so that your body language doesn't work against your goals. Providing a true barometer of your feelings and attitudes is the single greatest benefit of purposeful, effective physical action in public speaking. There are other benefits as well. • Physical actions make messages more meaningful. • People tend to become bored with things that don't move. They will naturally look at moving objects. • Audiences remember messages that reach multiple senses. Therefore gestures, body movements, and facial expressions are valuable tools when employed skillfully. • Physical actions punctuate your speeches. Written language includes an array of punctuation marks: commas, semicolons, periods, question marks, 10 Days to More Confident Public Speaking 102 exclamation points, and so on. However, when you speak, you use an entirely different set of symbols to show what part of your speech is most important and to add power and vitality to your words. • Physical actions help relieve nervous tension. Being nervous before a speech is healthy. It shows that your speech is important to you. But using your body effectively can help dispel your nervousness once you start speaking. Proper Speaking Posture How you position your body when you speak communicates a set of visual messages to an audience. Good posture also helps you breathe properly and project your voice effectively. When you stand still, be careful not to sway or rock. Make sure both feet are planted firmly on the floor and your shoulders are square. Don't lean, slouch, or hunch over. When you walk, stand tall. Be proud of yourself—you have an important message to communicate! Gestures Gestures are specific body movements that reinforce a verbal message. Most gestures are made with your hands and arms. Your hands are marvelous tools of communication. A speaker's gestures can suggest very precise bits of meaning to an audience. To be effective, a speaker's gestures must be purposeful. They must also have the same meaning to the audience as they do to the speaker. Gestures reflect not only what is being said, but the personality behind the message. 103 Say It with Style • Gestures clarify and support your words. They strengthen the audience's understanding of your verbal message. • Gestures dramatize your ideas. They help paint vivid pictures in your listeners' minds. • Gestures lend emphasis and vitality. They underscore your feelings and attitudes. • Gestures help dissipate nervous tension. They are a good outlet for nervous energy. • Gestures function as visual aids. They enhance audience attentiveness and retention. • Gestures stimulate audience participation. They help elicit the response you want. Gestures are grouped into four categories: 1. Descriptive gestures. Are used to clarify or enhance. Some descriptive gestures include using your hands to indicate the size, shape, location, and function of something, like choppy ocean waves, a huge mountain, or a miniature creature. 2. Emphatic gestures. Underscore what is being said. For example, a clenched fist suggests strong feelings such as anger or determination. 3. Suggestive gestures. Are symbols of ideas or emotions. For example, an open palm suggests giving or receiving, while a shrug of the shoulders indicates ignorance, perplexity, or irony. 4. Prompting gestures. Are used to evoke a desired response from the audience. For example, if you want your listeners to raise their hands, applaud, or perform some other action, you will encourage the desired response by doing the act yourself as an example. 10 Days to More Confident Public Speaking 104 Location of Gestures You can make gestures above, below, or at or near your shoulders; each position produces a different effect on your speech delivery. 1. Gestures above the shoulders suggest physical height, inspiration, or emotion. 2. Gestures below the shoulders indicate sadness, rejection, apathy, or condemnation. 3. Gestures at or near the shoulders suggest calmness, serenity. The most frequently used gesture involves an open palm held outward toward the audience. As I said earlier, holding your palm outward implies giving or receiving. Unfortunately, most speakers use this gesture unconsciously as a general movement without any specific meaning. A palm held downward expresses suppression, secrecy, completion, or stability. A palm held upward and outward suggests stopping. Hands also imply measurement such as tall, short, small, long, and so on. As you practice your speech, experiment with different gestures to find those that both feel natural to you and underscore your message. Don't Keep Your Hands to Yourself

There are speakers who, with a well-placed gesture, can move an audience to the edge of their seats. For many speakers, however, the only body movements included in their presentations are the frantic clutching of note cards and grasping the lectern for support. Body movement and gestures make or break a speech. You can motivate your audience through welltimed gestures, pacing, and, of course, eye contact. Gestures should consist of purposeful movements of the 105 Say It with Style head, shoulders, arms, hands, and entire body. They should not be too repetitive. All too often, when men stand up to speak, they immediately put their hands in their pockets. As they continue the presentation, their hands go deeper and deeper. When they eventually try to use their hands to gesture naturally, they find they're so deep in their pockets that they have difficulty getting them out. Men also have the habit of playing with their pocket change. This only draws your audience's attention to your hands and pockets and distracts them from listening to your message. Women, on the other hand, have a habit of playing with their jewelry, hair, or clothes. For example, tugging at an earring, brushing their hair back with their fingers, or pulling their suit jacket down. Each of these habits is distracting to your audience. International speaker David Peoples provides this list of distractions that are guaranteed to take the audience's attention off the subject. • Rattling keys or coins in your pocket • Using ums, uhs, and ya knows • Sucking the teeth • Twisting a ring • Stroking a beard • Lip licking • Lip biting • Tugging your ear • Cracking your knuckles • Pushing your glasses back on the bridge of your nose • Playing with a watch

• Drumming your fingers • Bouncing a pencil on its eraser • Blowing hair out of your eyes • Popping the top of a marker • Extending and retracting a telescopic pointer • Twirling hair • Playing with beads, gold chains, or other jewelry When a gesture is not necessary, make sure you have a natural resting place for your hands, such as by your side, or with the elbows slightly bent and hands at waist level, in preparation for your next gesture. How to Gesture Effectively Gestures are reflections of every speaker's individual personality. What's right for one speaker may not be right for another; however, if you apply the following seven rules, you can become a dynamic, confident speaker who uses gestures well. 1. Respond naturally to what you think, feel, and see. It's natural for you to gesture. If you inhibit your impulse to gesture, you'll probably become tense. 2. Create the condition for gesturing, not the gesture. When you speak, you should be totally involved in communicating—not thinking about your hands. Your gestures should be naturally motivated by the content of your presentation. 3. Suit the action to the word and the occasion. Your visual and verbal messages must function as partners in communicating the same thought or feeling. Every gesture you make should be purposeful and reflective of 107 Say It with Style your words so the audience will note only the effect, not the gesture itself. 4. Don't overdo the gesturing. You'll draw the listener away from your message. Young audiences are usually attracted to a speaker who uses vigorous gestures, but older, more conservative groups may feel your physical actions are overwhelming or irritating. 5. Make your gestures convincing. Your gestures need to be lively and distinct if they are to convey the intended impressions. Effective gestures are vigorous enough to be convincing yet slow enough and broad enough to be clearly visible without being overpowering. For example, if you are conveying excitement about a point or topic in your speech, show it in your face such as with a big smile. If you are excited and don't show it, your body language sends a negative message. Your gestures need to match your words and the mood you are conveying. 6. Make your gestures smooth and well timed. This rule is the most important but also the hardest. Why? Gestures have to be planned in advance so you can incorporate them during your speech rehearsal. In addition, practice sessions allow you to get a sense of how early you need to start your gesture so it coincides with the point you are making. Every gesture has three parts: • The approach. Your body begins to move in anticipation. • The stroke.The gesture itself. • The return.This brings your body back to a balanced posture. 10 Days to More Confident Public Speaking 108 The flow of a gesture—the approach, the stroke, the return—most be smoothly executed so that only the stroke is evident to the audience. While it's advisable to practice gesturing, don't try to memorize your every move. This makes your gesturing stilted and ineffective. For example, you're standing on the left-hand side of the stage (the audience's left) and you need to use the flip chart to illustrate a point, but the flip chart is on the far right-hand side of the stage (the audience's right). You may say to your audience, "Let's take a look at it on the flip chart." As you start this statement begin walking toward the flip chart (the approach). Your goal is to start your gesture early enough so you can walk naturally toward the flip chart. At the word flip chart place your hand on the flip chart. This combined walking and placement of your hand on the flip chart is the gesture or the stroke. After a brief moment, place your hand on the flip chart and then take your hand and move it to one of your resting positions. This is the return or completion of the gesture. 7. Make natural, spontaneous gesturing a habit. The first step in becoming adept at gesturing is to determine what, if anything, you are doing now. For example, pay attention to the gestures you use in everyday conversations and try to use these gestures during your presentation. If you prefer, you can videotape your practice speech. For more on videotaping, see Day 8 and "Body Language" later in this chapter. The camcorder is truthful and unforgiving. If you want to become a more effective speaker, you need to make the camcorder your best friend. Recording yourself is a surefire way to eliminate your distracting mannerisms. 109 Say It with Style Videotape yourself and identify your bad habits. Then work at eliminating them. To improve gestures, practice—but never during a speech. Practice gesturing when speaking informally to friends, family members, and co-workers. Body Movement/Walking Patterns Changing your position or location while speaking is the broadest, most visible physical action you can perform. Therefore it can either help drive your message home or spell failure for even the most well-planned speech. Moving your body in a controlled, purposeful manner creates three benefits. 1. Supports and reinforces what you say 2. Attracts an audience's attention 3. Burns up nervous energy and relieves physical tension However, body movement can work against you. Remember this one rule: Never move without a reason. As I said earlier, the eye is inevitably attracted to a moving object, so any body movement you make during a speech invites attention. Too much movement, even the right kind, can become distracting to an audience. Bear in mind the following types of body movement: • Stepping forward during a speech suggests you are arriving at an important point. • Stepping backward indicates you've concluded an idea and want the audience to relax for a moment. 10 Days to More Confident Public Speaking 110 • Lateral movement implies a transition; it indicates that you are leaving one thought and taking up another. For example, if you are standing in front of the audience and are ready to move on to your next point, move slowly sideways until you are standing next to the lectern. The final reason for body movement is the easiest: to get from one place to another. In almost every speaking situation, you must walk from the location you are addressing your audience to your props, especially if you use visual aids. Always change positions by leading with the foot nearest your destination. You may ask, Why move in the first place? Moving forces people to focus and follow you. The way you walk from your seat to the speaker's location is very important. When you are introduced, you should appear eager to speak. Many speakers look as though they are heading toward execution. • Walk confidently from your seat to the lectern. Pause there a few seconds and then move out from behind the lectern. As discussed before, it is wise to use the lectern as a point of departure, not a barrier to hide behind. • Smile before you say your first words. • Don't stand too close or move beyond the first row of participants. • Don't walk too much. It works against you. Continuous pacing is distracting. • Walking stresses an important idea. It is essential that you walk with purpose and intention, not just a random shift of position. For example, taking about three steps, moving at a slight angle, usually works best. 111 Say It with Style • Use three positions with visual aids. Your "home" position is front and center. The other two positions should be relatively near the "home" position. You can move to the right of the podium and then to the left. Using and varying these three positions prevents you from favoring one side of the audience. If you're speaking on a stage, these three positions are called front center, stage left, and stage right. Never stand in front of any visual aid. • Practice your walking patterns to and from your three positions. These positions should be planned just as your hand gestures are. For example, you want your body to move and gesture naturally. However, since most people are nervous about speaking in public, they tend to stiffen their muscles and hold back their natural tendency to gesture. Let your body tell you when it wants to move. • Maintain good posture when you are not moving. Tips You Must Know About Facial Expressions Leave that deadpan expression to poker players. A good speaker realizes that appropriate facial expressions are an important part of effective communication. In fact, facial expressions are often the key determinant of the meaning behind the message. People watch a speaker's face during a presentation. When you speak, your face—more clearly than any other part of your body—communicates to your audience your attitudes, feelings, and emotions. Dr. Paul Ekman of the University of California at San Francisco has made a career of studying facial expression and 10 Days to More Confident Public Speaking 112 facial animation. He mapped out a technique for coding facial expressions called facial action coding system, FACS, based on the role facial muscles play in expressing different emotions. Ekman's research indicates that there are seven emotional expressions shared by everyone: sadness, happiness, anger, interest, fear, contempt, and surprise. Here is a list of tips you need to know: 1. Be yourself. Don't try to copy the facial expression style of someone else. For example, just because your favorite professional speaker starts his or her presentations by telling a story using exaggerated facial expressions doesn't mean it will work for you. 2. Don't overdo it. Some people intentionally try to control their facial expressions by forcing themselves to smile or use another expression that isn't natural to them. Watch out for "fake" facial expressions that have a negative impact on your speech or compromise your sincerity. 3. Practice in front of a mirror. Notice what expressions you use while speaking. Study how to control your facial expressions. Ask yourself, Do they match my words? 4. Create different moods. While practicing in front of the mirror, see if your facial expressions convey the mood you want to create. If your face isn't showing any emotion, stop, refocus, and try again. 5. Think about what you are saying. Focus on your message and communicating with your audience, and your facial expressions follow. 6. Smile before you begin. As I've said before, the one true international nonverbal expression understood by all is the smile. A warm smile before you begin to speak 113 Say It with Style warms up an audience quickly, and ending with a smile puts your audience at ease with what they've just learned. Eye Contact One key element of facial expression is eye contact. It is estimated that 80 percent of nonverbal communication takes place with your face and your eyes. Eye contact is the cement that binds together speakers and their audiences. When you speak, your eyes involve your listeners in your presentation. There is no faster way to break a communication bond between you and the audience than by failing to look at your listeners. No matter the size of your audience, each listener wants to feel that you are talking directly to him or her. Looking at your listeners as individuals convinces them that you are sincere, are interested in them, and care whether or not they accept your message. Effective eye contact is also an important feedback device that makes the speaking situation a two-way communication process. By looking at your audience, you determine how they are reacting to your presentation. How to Use Your Eyes Effectively Your eyes convey a message to your audience. Here are tips to help you use your eyes to better communicate with your audience. • Know your material. Know your material backward and forward, so you don't have to devote mental energy to scanning your note cards for the next topic (an audience interprets this latter behavior negatively, 10 Days to More Confident Public Speaking 114 perceiving that you are unsure about what follows your last point). Prepare well and rehearse often so you don't have to depend heavily on notes. • Establish a visual bond. Select one person and maintain eye contact with that person long enough to establish a visual bond, about five to ten seconds. Then shift your gaze to another person. In a small group, this is relatively easy. With larger crowds it's difficult. Instead select one or two individuals in each section of the room and establish personal bonds with them. This will leave each listener with the impression you're talking directly to him or her. • Monitor visual feedback. While you are talking, your listeners are responding with their own nonverbal messages such as a smile or nod of the head. Use your eyes to seek out this valuable feedback. If individuals aren't looking at you, they may not be listening, either. Reasons for this include the following: —They can't hear you. Solution: If you are not using a microphone, speak louder. —They are bored. Solution: Use humor, increase your vocal variety, or add powerful gestures or body movements. —They are puzzled. Solution: Repeat or rephrase what you have just said. —They are fidgeting nervously. Solution: You may be using distracting mannerisms. Heighten your selfawareness of your voice and body language. On the other hand, if your listeners' faces indicate interest and close attention, don't change a thing. You're doing a great job! 115 Say It with Style Your Overall Appearance Wear your best suit or dress for your presentation, the outfit that elicits the most compliments. Make sure that every item of clothing is clean, pressed, and tailored. You know what type of attire to wear based on the information you learned from your preprogram and custom survey (Day 3) about your audience. Don't wear jewelry that might glitter or jingle when you move or gesture. This diverts attention from your speech. For the same reason, remove items and anything such as pocket change that makes noise when you move. The first impression you give is completely related to your overall appearance and occurs even before you are introduced to deliver your speech. To convey a positive appearance as the audience arrives, you shouldn't be studying your speech, but rather mingling with the audience and projecting that same friendly, confident attitude you will use in your speech. Body Language Here are three ways to make your body speak effectively. 1. Rid yourself of distracting mannerisms. When your actions are intertwined with your words, the impact of your speech is strengthened. If your platform behavior includes mannerisms unrelated to your spoken message, those actions call attention to themselves and away from your speech. Eliminate vocal and visual impediments. You can easily correct a verbal mistake because you hear your own words. Since you can't see yourself, most distracting mannerisms go uncorrected. You can't eliminate them unless you know they exist. Again, the 10 Days to More Confident Public Speaking 116 best way to correct this behavior is to videotape yourself. Here is my four-step process for reviewing your videotape to free yourself of physical behaviors that distract from your speech: • Review #1. Review your tape without looking for mannerisms. Just listen to the presentation and evaluate the overall impact you experience from watching the tape. • Review #2.Turn the volume down and review your tape a second time. Look for visual distractions such as swaying your body, fixing your hair, or touching your face. Take notes on what you observe—note distracting mannerisms as well as gestures or other body movements that you feel work well. • Review #3.Turn the picture off or turn away from the screen and listen only to your voice.The audience interprets and makes assumptions about your body language based on your verbal interpretations. Become accustomed to listening to your own voice. Get to know it as others hear it. Note what you like and dislike. Pay attention to the speed, volume, and the tone of your voice. • Review #4. After you complete your list of distracting mannerisms and your more positive points, ask one or two family members to watch the tape with you. Get their initial impression. Ask them to be honest about the strengths and weaknesses of your mannerisms. A great way to practice overcoming your distracting mannerisms is to pay attention to your mannerisms the next several times you have a conversation with a friend or family member. 117 Say It with Style 2. Let your body mirror your message. If you are interested in your subject, believe what you are saying, and want to share your message with others, your physical movements come from within and are appropriate to what you are saying. For example, I was working with a company CEO who believed he shouldn't use his hands to communicate because he was Italian and felt he already "talked" too much with his hands. As a result of this belief, he intentionally restricted his movements and hand gestures. Subconsciously he created an image he felt he needed to protect and he put on a mask by not allowing his inner self to truly express what he was feeling. After working with him on this behavior and teaching him how to speak conversationally using hand gestures, I was able to fine-tune his gestures so they were more effective in communicating his message. To become an effective speaker, it is essential that you throw away your mask and share your true feelings with your audience. Your audience wants to know how you feel about your subject. If you want to convince others, you must convey your convictions. Remember this credo: Speak from the heart and to the soul. 3. Use your everyday speaking situations to practice body language. Whenever you speak to people, make an extra effort to notice how you speak. Observe your listener's facial expressions to see if he or she does or does not comprehend what you are saying. For example, a listener who is not making eye contact with you may not understand or may be bored. A listener who responds to your message, such as with a nod of 10 Days to More Confident Public Speaking 118 agreement, understands and is attentive to your presentation. As an exercise to help you practice body language and gestures, prepare a ninety-second presentation about yourself. Describe who you are and what you do. Record your presentation and review it using the four-point process discussed in step one. Since you are talking about yourself, no research is required; however, you do need to prepare what you are going to say and how you are going to say it. Plan everything, including your gestures and walking patterns. Confidence Builder: Voice Tips Guaranteed to Entrance Your Audience No matter what you believe, there is no such thing as the "perfect voice." Each individual voice is as unique as the person's hairstyle and manner of dress. Nothing is worse than listening to a speaker with a monotone voice. While your visual presentation has a big impact on your audience, your tone of voice is also very important. How you sound and the manner in which you vary your voice has a notable effect on your listeners. Top Ten List: Tips for Creating a Confident Voice • Have a conversation with your audience. Think about your message, and just think of your speech as having a conversation with your audience. For example, think of your audience as a friend you talk to often. 119 Say It with Style • Talk loudly enough. Make sure that your audience can hear you. Use a microphone if necessary. If the audience cannot hear you, they will tune you out. • Use expression in your voice. If you truly believe in what you are saying, this will communicate through the expression in your voice. • Pronounce your words carefully. Take the time to learn proper pronunciation. Nothing is worse than watching a speaker stumble over words. • Do not speak too fast. This is one of the most common problems speakers have. Many people speak too fast because of nervousness. Watch your speed! • Do not use filler words such as "um," "ah," or "okay." Spend time and learn to eliminate these filler words. • Increase your volume to convey excitement. Show excitement in your voice, but be careful not to yell. • Decrease your volume to evoke emotion. Lowering your volume is an effective way to show your emotions. Just be careful not to speak too softly. • Change your speed to match your audience's needs. I speak to a variety of age groups ranging from older adults to elementary students. In general, with older groups I speak more slowly. Since I usually speak on the faster side, this is a challenge for me. A younger audience, on the other hand, looks for fast-paced presentations and a speaker who demonstrates high energy. I also use speed to "wake up" an audience. If a previous speaker has effectively put the audience to sleep, I use speed to reenergize them. I use this speed in connection with animated movement, but I make sure I 10 Days to More Confident Public Speaking 120 still speak clearly so the audience understands my message. • Use proper breathing. Inhale and exhale fully to assure that you project your voice clearly and provide the necessary air support to your voice.

CHAPTER SEVEN

EFFICIENCY THROUGH OF PITCH

Speech is simply a modified form of singing: the principal difference being in the fact that in singing the vowel sounds are prolonged and the intervals are short, whereas in speech the words are uttered in what may be called "staccato" tones, the vowels not being specially prolonged and the intervals between the words being more distinct. The fact that in singing we have a larger range of tones does not properly distinguish it from ordinary speech. In speech we have likewise a variation of tones, and even in ordinary conversation there is a difference of from three to six semi-tones, as I have found in my investigations, and in some persons the range is as high as one octave. --WILLIAM SCHEPPEGRELL, Popular Science Monthly. By pitch, as everyone knows, we mean the relative position of a vocal tone--as, high, medium, low, or any variation between. In public speech we apply it not only to a single utterance, as an exclamation or a monosyllable (Oh! or the) but to any group of syllables, words, and even sentences that may be spoken in a single tone. This distinction it is important to keep in mind, for the efficient speaker not only changes the pitch of successive syllables (see Chapter VII, "Efficiency through Inflection"), but gives a different pitch to different parts, or word-groups, of successive sentences. It is this phase of the subject which we are considering in this chapter. Every Change in the Thought Demands a Change in the Voice-Pitch Whether the speaker follows the rule consciously, unconsciously, or subconsciously, this is the logical basis upon which all good voice variation is made, yet this law is violated more often than any other by public speakers. A criminal may disregard a law of the state without detection and punishment, but the speaker who violates this regulation suffers its penalty at once in his loss of effectiveness, while his innocent hearers must endure the monotony--

for monotony is not only a sin of the perpetrator, as we have shown, but a plague on the victims as well. Change of pitch is a stumbling block for almost all beginners, and for many experienced speakers also. This is especially true when the words of the speech have been memorized. If you wish to hear how pitch-monotony sounds, strike the same note on the piano over and over again. You have in your speaking voice a range of pitch from high to low, with a great many shades between the extremes. With all these notes available there is no excuse for offending the ears and taste of your audience by continually using the one note. True, the reiteration of the same tone in music--as in pedal point on an organ composition--may be made the foundation of beauty, for the harmony weaving about that one basic tone produces a consistent, insistent quality not felt in pure variety of chord sequences. In like manner the intoning voice in a ritual may--though it rarely does--possess a solemn beauty. But the public speaker should shun the monotone as he would a pestilence. Continual Change of Pitch is Nature's Highest Method In our search for the principles of efficiency we must continually go back to nature. Listen--really listen--to the birds sing. Which of these feathered tribes are most pleasing in their vocal efforts: those whose voices, though sweet, have little or no range, or those that, like the canary, the lark, and the nightingale, not only possess a considerable range but utter their notes in continual variety of combinations? Even a sweet-toned chirp, when reiterated without change, may grow maddening to the enforced listener. CHAPTER IV 19 The little child seldom speaks in a monotonous pitch. Observe the conversations of little folk that you hear on the street or in the home, and note the continual changes of pitch. The unconscious speech of most adults is likewise full of pleasing variations. Imagine someone speaking the following, and consider if the effect would not be just about as indicated. Remember, we are not now discussing the inflection of single words, but the general pitch in which phrases are spoken. (High pitch) "I'd like to leave for my vacation tomorrow,--(lower) still, I have so much to do. (Higher) Yet I suppose if I wait until I have time I'll never go." Repeat this, first in the pitches indicated, and then all in the one pitch, as many speakers would. Observe the difference in naturalness of effect. The following exercise should be spoken in a purely conversational tone, with numerous changes of pitch. Practise it until your delivery would cause a stranger in the next room to think you were discussing an actual incident with a friend, instead of delivering a memorized monologue. If you are in doubt about the effect you have secured, repeat it to a friend and ask him if it sounds like memorized words. If it does, it is wrong.

Jack, I hear you've gone and done it.--Yes, I know; most fellows will; went and tried it once myself, sir, though you see I'm single still. And you met her--did you tell me--down at Newport, last July, and resolved to ask the question at a soirée? So did I. I suppose you left the ball-room, with its music and its light; for they say love's flame is brightest in the darkness of the night. Well, you walked along together, overhead the starlit sky; and I'll bet--old man, confess it--you were frightened. So was I. So you strolled along the terrace, saw the summer moonlight pour all its radiance on the waters, as they rippled on the shore, till at length you gathered courage, when you saw that none was nigh--did you draw her close and tell her that you loved her? So did I. Well, I needn't ask you further, and I'm sure I wish you joy. Think I'll wander down and see you when you're married--eh, my boy? When the honeymoon is over and you're settled down, we'll try-- What? the deuce you say! Rejected--you rejected? So was I. --Anonymous. The necessity for changing pitch is so self-evident that it should be grasped and applied immediately. However, it requires patient drill to free yourself from monotony of pitch. In natural conversation you think of an idea first, and then find words to express it. In memorized speeches you are liable to speak the words, and then think what they mean--and many speakers seem to trouble very little even about that. Is it any wonder that reversing the process should reverse the result? Get back to nature in your methods of expression. Read the following selection in a nonchalant manner, never pausing to think what the words really mean. Try it again, carefully studying the thought you have assimilated. Believe the idea, desire to express it effectively, and imagine an audience before you. Look them earnestly in the face and repeat this truth. If you follow directions, you will note that you have made many changes of pitch after several readings. CHAPTER IV 20 It is not work that kills men; it is worry. Work is healthy; you can hardly put more upon a man than he can bear. Worry is rust upon the blade. It is not the revolution that destroys the machinery but the friction. --HENRY WARD BEECHER. Change of Pitch Produces Emphasis This is a highly important statement. Variety in pitch maintains the hearer's interest, but one of the surest ways to compel attention--to secure unusual emphasis-- is to change the pitch of your voice suddenly and in a marked degree. A great contrast always arouses attention. White shows whiter against black; a cannon roars louder in the Sahara silence than in the Chicago hurly burly--

these are simple illustrations of the power of contrast. "What is Congress going to do next? ---------------------------------- (High pitch) | | | I do not know." ----------------- (Low pitch) By such sudden change of pitch during a sermon Dr. Newell Dwight Hillis recently achieved great emphasis and suggested the gravity of the question he had raised. The foregoing order of pitch-change might be reversed with equally good effect, though with a slight change in seriousness--either method produces emphasis when used intelligently, that is, with a common-sense appreciation of the sort of emphasis to be attained. In attempting these contrasts of pitch it is important to avoid unpleasant extremes. Most speakers pitch their voices too high. One of the secrets of Mr. Bryan's eloquence is his low, bell-like voice. Shakespeare said that a soft, gentle, low voice was "an excellent thing in woman;" it is no less so in man, for a voice need not be blatant to be powerful,--and must not be, to be pleasing. In closing, let us emphasize anew the importance of using variety of pitch. You sing up and down the scale, first touching one note and then another above or below it. Do likewise in speaking. Thought and individual taste must generally be your guide as to where to use a low, a moderate, or a high pitch.

KNOWING THE PRICE WE MUST PAY, THE SACRIFICE WE MUST MAKE, THE BURDENS WE MUST CARRY, THE ASSAULTS WE MUST ENDURE--KNOWING FULL WELL THE COST--yet we enlist, and we enlist for the war. FOR WE KNOW THE JUSTICE OF OUR CAUSE, and we know, too, its certain triumph. NOT RELUCTANTLY THEN, but eagerly, not with faint hearts BUT STRONG, do we now advance upon the enemies of the people. FOR THE CALL THAT COMES TO US is the call that came to our fathers. As they responded so shall we. "HE HATH SOUNDED FORTH A TRUMPET that shall never call retreat. HE IS SIFTING OUT THE HEARTS OF MEN before His judgment seat. OH, BE SWIFT OUR SOULS TO ANSWER HIM, BE JUBILANT OUR FEET, Our God is marching on." --ALBERT J. BEVERIDGE. Remember that two sentences, or two parts of the same sentence, which contain changes of thought, cannot possibly be given effectively in the same key. Let us repeat, every big change of thought requires a big change of pitch. What the beginning student will think are big changes of pitch will be monotonously alike. Learn to speak some thoughts in a very high tone--others in a very, very low tone. DEVELOP RANGE. It is almost impossible to use too much of it.

Hear how he clears the points o' Faith Wi' rattlin' an' thumpin'! Now meekly calm, now wild in wrath, He's stampin' an' he's jumpin'. --ROBERT

BURNS, Holy Fair. The Latins have bequeathed to us a word that has no precise equivalent in our tongue, therefore we have accepted it, body unchanged--it is the word tempo, and means rate of movement, as measured by the time consumed in executing that movement. Thus far its use has been largely limited to the vocal and musical arts, but it would not be surprising to hear tempo applied to more concrete matters, for it perfectly illustrates the real meaning of the word to say that an ox-cart moves in slow tempo, an express train in a fast tempo. Our guns that fire six hundred times a minute, shoot at a fast tempo; the old muzzle loader that required three minutes to load, shot at a slow tempo. Every musician understands this principle: it requires longer to sing a half note than it does an eighth note. Now tempo is a tremendously important element in good platform work, for when a speaker delivers a whole address at very nearly the same rate of speed he is depriving himself of one of his chief means of emphasis and power. The baseball pitcher, the bowler in cricket, the tennis server, all know the value of change of pace--change of tempo--in delivering their ball, and so must the public speaker observe its power. Change of Tempo Lends Naturalness to the Delivery Naturalness, or at least seeming naturalness, as was explained in the chapter on "Monotony," is greatly to be desired, and a continual change of tempo will go a long way towards establishing it. Mr. Howard Lindsay, Stage Manager for Miss Margaret Anglin, recently said to the present writer that change of pace was one of the most effective tools of the actor. While it must be admitted that the stilted mouthings of many actors indicate cloudy mirrors, still the public speaker would do well to study the actor's use of tempo. There is, however, a more fundamental and effective source at which to study naturalness--a trait which, once lost, is shy of recapture: that source is the common conversation of any well-bred circle. This is the standard we strive to reach on both stage and platform--with certain differences, of course, which will appear as we go on. If speaker and actor were to reproduce with absolute fidelity every variation of utterance--every whisper, grunt, pause, silence, and explosion--of conversation as we find it typically in everyday life, much of the interest would leave the public utterance. Naturalness in public address is something more than faithful reproduction of nature--it is the reproduction of those typical parts of nature's work which are truly representative of the whole. The realistic story-writer understands this in writing dialogue, and we must take it into account in seeking for naturalness through change of tempo. Suppose you speak the first of the following sentences in a slow tempo, the second quickly, observing how natural is the effect. Then speak both with the same rapidity and note the difference. I can't recall what I did with my knife. Oh, now I remember I gave it to Mary. We see here that a change of tempo often occurs in the same sentence--for tempo applies not only to single words, groups of words, and groups of sentences, but to the major parts of a public speech as well.

CHAPTER EIGHT

Ethics and Language

Today I will focus on the language of giving speeches. Speech language includes elements such as the following: • alliteration • clichés • metaphors and similes • imagery How you incorporate the various language components depends on your own speaking style and comfort level. As a professional speaker, I write speeches for business professionals, but I have also been hired to write speeches for brides, bridegrooms, best men, teachers, administrators, politicians, and even ministers. Although the written style for each is unique, all my clients ask that their speeches come across as conversational. Being able to write conversationally can be a challenge, but with a strong working knowledge of the range of language elements at your disposal, it does get easier.The Elements of Language Let's look at the various elements of language and some tips to help you use them in each of your speeches. However, avoid overuse of these elements because they can become distractions for your audience and may steer them away from listening to your message. Alliteration An alliteration is a sentence or long phrase in which each of the words begins with the same letter. Two common alliterations most of you are familiar with are "She sells seashells by the seashore" and "Peter Piper picked a peck of pickled peppers." Alliteration can be used to make a point memorable in your presentation or to convey dramatic or poetic nuances. This technique also gives the listener a catchy phrase to remember a particular message. The following examples use this repeated letter technique. Think about how you can use alliteration in your speeches and presentations. Have fun with it. In my workshops I use an alliteration I call the nine P's: Prior Proper Preparations Prevents Poor Performance of the Person Putting on the Presentation. Another alliteration I use represents the three R's of motivation: • Recognition • Reward • Reinforcement Clichés Clichés are short, trite phrases that refer to commonly held ideas but have lost their originality owing to overuse. "Look 10 Days to More Confident Public Speaking 124 on the bright side" is one example of a cliché. Here are several others: • Live and learn. • What goes around comes around. • Don't worry, be happy. • Today is the first day of the rest of your life. • No pain, no gain. • Every cloud has a silver lining. • Every rose has its thorn. • Cheer up, it's not the end of the world. • It could be worse. You get the idea. Using clichés in your speeches is very effective as long as they fit with your message. For example, if you are giving a motivational speech to a group of people starting a new exercise program, the cliché "No pain, no gain" may very well be appropriate to use. One cliché I use when working with clients who are uncomfortable speaking in front of people is "Cheer up, it's not the end of the world." I explain to the client that he must conquer his fear of public speaking and believe that the audience will like him and be interested in his message. Metaphors and Similes A metaphor is a figurative comparison between two usually unconnected things, resulting in an image in the mind's eye. For example, the statement "My love is a rose" is a metaphor. The message the listener gets is that, like a rose, love is fragile and beautiful yet thorny. Like a metaphor, a simile is a figure of speech where two usually unconnected things are compared, often in a phrase 125 Language and Ethics introduced by "like" or "as." For example, "My love is like a red, red rose." It is common to use metaphors or similes to express feelings, ideas, and concepts that are complex or hold a special meaning for you, or to paint a particular, even humorous, image for the audience. In a motivational speech to get a participant to feel good about him- or herself, I used the simile "You look like a million bucks." Exercise: Metaphor or Simile Come up with a metaphor or simile to describe how you might feel in the following situations. 1. Getting an A on a final exam when you would have been happy to have gotten a C. 2. Your first experience of speaking anxiety or stage fright. 3. Witnessing a serious accident. Imagery Imagery is the use of vivid or figurative language to represent objects, actions, or ideas. In seminars I use imagery to tell a story. Imagery is a wonderful technique to help you convey your message and help individuals "picture" abstract concepts. Also, I use imagery to help clients have more self-confidence and self-esteem when they are preparing to speak in front of a group of people. When I use imagery in my presentations I use three objects related to my topic and describe each. For example, let's say your topic is job hunting and you decide to use imagery to discuss the job interview process and three types of job candidates. Here are three images you might choose to use to describe these candidates: 10 Days to More Confident Public Speaking 126 • Overkill. The individual who arrives at the job interview wearing an extremely expensive suit, with his hair slicked back, and carrying an attaché case, laptop, and cell phone. • Professional. The individual who arrives at the interview ten minutes early wearing a clean, wellpressed, fashionable but conservative suit, with her hair neatly swept off her face, and carrying a slim portfolio and small purse. • Laid back. The individual who strolls into the interview fifteen minutes late wearing wrinkled pants and an untucked, collarless shirt, with his hair unkempt, scraggly facial hair, and holding a dog-eared resume in his hand. Danger Zone: Ethics In preparing any speech it is crucial to develop and use your own material. It is unethical to use someone else's stories, data, or research and try to pass it off as your own. Using unattributed material is called plagiarism and is illegal. If you develop and use your own material, you won't find yourself on the wrong end of a lawsuit. If you do, however, find information or data from another source that supports your claim or ideas, you can get the author's permission in writing before you use the information, or if it's from a research study or professional journal you can attribute the information in a verbal citation in your speech. For example, "According to data by the Gallup Organization . . ." It is unethical to use other people's material (even something by a colleague) without • asking them. • giving proper credit in the speech. 127 Language and Ethics I continually receive calls from businesses, colleges, and authors asking for permission to reprint one of my articles. In return I expect proper credit. In my career as a public speaker, I have experienced only a few incidences when an individual has actually taken my articles word for word and tried to pass them off as his or her own. This is not only unethical, but also in violation of copyright laws. Positive Performance: What You Need to Know About Plagiarism Northwestern University's "Principles Regarding Academic Integrity" defines plagiarism to its students as "submitting material that in part or whole is not entirely [the writer's or speaker's] own work without attributing those same portions to their correct source." Plagiarism occurs in many forms other than writing, such as art, music, computer code, mathematics, and scientific work. To help you, here are Northwestern University's guidelines for proper attribution. Guidelines for Proper Attribution As you plan a speech, you will likely draw from a vast pool of texts, ideas, and findings that individuals have accumulated over hundreds, even thousands, of years. What you call originality is actually the innovative combining, amending, or extending of material from that pool. The most helpful form of attribution is a citation where you give precise information about your source: where the material came from, the author's name, and the publication date. At times it is difficult to know what needs to be cited. 10 Days to More Confident Public Speaking 128 Common knowledge or ideas that have been in the public domain and are found in a number of sources don't need to be cited. One example of a document that doesn't require a citation is the Bill of Rights. If you are in doubt, document. As someone who is learning to develop your own speaking style, you may want to emulate your favorite professional speaker and copy certain styles and techniques. Professional speakers, myself included, are very sensitive to having individuals use our personal stories in their seminar or keynote address. Develop your own stories that can relate to your message. • Learn when to give proper attribution. An attribution is necessary in a speech when something you say might leave listeners in doubt about whom you are attributing the material to and for what reason. • Respect the source. Make sure your attribution expresses your appreciation for being allowed to borrow the information. For example, at the end of your speech you could say to the audience, "I would like to take this opportunity to thank Herb Johnson for his compelling work in the area of foster care in inner cities." Top Ten List: Influential and Memorable Speeches in History Following are what I believe to be the ten most influential and memorable speeches in history. Notice that I have not included entire speeches, just excerpts. 1. The Gettysburg Address. By Abraham Lincoln on November 19, 1863. "Four score and seven years ago, our fathers brought forth on this continent, a new 129 Language and Ethics nation, conceived in Liberty, and dedicated to the proposition that all men are created equal." I am sure you have read this address—one of the best-known speeches of American history—given by our sixteenth president during the Civil War. This speech is amazingly powerful even though it was only about two minutes long. Over time, the Gettysburg Address and its closing message—"government of the people, by the people, for the people"—have come to symbolize the definition of democracy itself. 2. Liberty or death. By Patrick Henry on March 23, 1775. Following the Boston Tea Party on December 16, 1773, in which American colonists dumped 342 chests of tea into Boston Harbor, the British Parliament enacted a series of so-called Intolerable Acts in response to the rebellion in Massachusetts. Henry's impassioned words "Forbid it, Almighty God! I know not what course others may take; but as for me, give me liberty or give me death!" influenced Virginia's government to support his resolutions, which in turn propelled Virginia into the American Revolution. 3. On women's right to vote. By Susan B. Anthony in 1873. In the 1880s women in the United States were legal underdogs who did not even have the right to vote. Susan B. Anthony gave a speech after she was arrested for casting an illegal vote in the presidential election of 1872. She was fined $100 but refused to pay. In her speech she stated, "Webster, Worcester, and Bouvier all define a citizen to be a person in the United States, entitled to vote and hold office. The only question left to be settled now is: Are women persons? And I hardly believe any of our opponents will have the hardihood to say they are not. Being persons, then, women are 10 Days to More Confident Public Speaking 130 citizens; and no state has a right to make any law, or to enforce any old law, that shall abridge their privileges or immunities. Hence, every discrimination against women in the constitution and laws of the several states is today null and void." Following her death in 1906 after decades of tireless work, both the Democratic and Republican parties endorsed women's right to vote. 4. "I have a dream." By Martin Luther King, August 28, 1963. King gave the keynote speech at the 1963 March on Washington for Jobs and Freedom, from the steps of the Lincoln Memorial, in front of about 250,000 people. Since 1963, King's "I have a dream" speech has become the most famous public address of the twentieth century. With his profound and far-reaching words, King cemented his place as a crusader for civil rights leadership. Here is the closing of his speech: "Let freedom ring. And when this happens, and when we allow freedom to ring—when we let it ring from every village and every hamlet, from every state and every city, we will be able to speed up that day when all of God's children—black men and white men, Jews and Gentiles, Protestants and Catholics—will be able to join hands and sing in the words of the old Negro spiritual: Free at last! Free at last! Thank God Almighty, we are free at last!" 5. For a declaration of war. By Franklin D. Roosevelt on December 8, 1941. On Sunday, December 7, 1941, the first assault wave of Japanese fighter planes attacked the U.S. naval base at Pearl Harbor, Hawaii, taking the Americans completely by surprise. On Monday, December 8, President Roosevelt appeared before 131 Language and Ethics Congress and made his speech asking for a declaration of war against Japan, calling the previous day "a date which will live in infamy": "I ask that Congress declare that since the unprovoked and dastardly attack by Japan on Sunday, December 7, 1941, a state of war has existed between the United States and the Japanese empire." 6. "We choose to go to the moon." By John F. Kennedy on September 12, 1962. In this 1962 speech made at Rice University in Houston, Texas, President John F. Kennedy reaffirmed America's commitment to landing a man on the moon before the end of the 1960s. The president spoke in philosophical terms about the need to solve the mysteries of space and also defended the enormous expense of the program. "Well, space is there, and we're going to climb it, and the moon and the planets are there, and new hopes for knowledge and peace are there. And, therefore, as we set sail we ask God's blessing on the most hazardous and dangerous and greatest adventure in which man has ever embarked." 7. "I am prepared to die." By Nelson Mandela on April 20, 1964. In 1962 Nelson Mandela was arrested by South African security police for his opposition to the white government and its apartheid ("separateness") policies of racial, political, and economic discrimination against the nonwhite majority. In 1964 the government brought further charges against Mandela, including sabotage, high treason, and conspiracy to overthrow the government. This was part of Mandela's statement at the opening of his defense trial in April 1964: "During my lifetime I have dedicated myself to this struggle of the African people. I have fought against white domination, and I have fought against black 10 Days to More Confident Public Speaking 132 domination. I have cherished the ideal of a democratic and free society in which all persons live together in harmony and with equal opportunities. It is an ideal which I hope to live for and to achieve. But if needs be, it is an ideal for which I am prepared to die." 8. "We shall overcome." By Lyndon B. Johnson on March 15, 1965. In this eloquent speech to Congress, President Lyndon B. Johnson used the phrase we shall overcome, borrowed from African American leaders struggling for equal rights. The speech came a week after deadly racial violence erupted in Selma, Alabama, as African Americans were attacked by police while preparing to march to Montgomery to protest voting rights discrimination. "What happened in Selma is part of a far larger movement which reaches into every section and state of America. It is the effort of American Negroes to secure for themselves the full blessings of American life. Their cause must be our cause too. Because it is not just Negroes, but really it is all of us, who must overcome the crippling legacy of bigotry and injustice. And we shall overcome." 9. Resigning the presidency. By Richard M. Nixon on August 8, 1974. A unique and tragic event in American politics occurred as President Richard M. Nixon spoke on TV in August of 1974 to the American public, announcing his decision to resign the presidency. Nixon's decision came after the Judiciary Committee of the House of Representatives voted to recommend his impeachment. During the Senate investigation, a Nixon aide revealed the president had installed a bugging system in the Oval Office that had recorded most conversations on tape. Under intense pressure in the spring of 1974, Nixon released edited transcripts of the 133 Language and Ethics tapes containing his conversations. "I have never been a quitter. To leave office before my term is completed is abhorrent to every instinct in my body. But as president, I must put the interest of America first. America needs a full-time president and a full-time Congress, particularly at this time with problems we face at home and abroad. . . . Therefore, I shall resign the presidency effective at noon tomorrow. . . ." 10. Recognition of the American Basketball League and the Women's National Basketball Association. By Congresswoman Corrine Brown on June 17, 1997. Congresswoman Corrine Brown gave this speech before Congress, asking them to sign a bill acknowledging the establishment of two new women's professional basketball leagues: the American Basketball League (ABL) and the Women's National Basketball Association (WNBA). "The success of women's sports has proved that America is ready for women's professional basketball. We have built a generation of talented players who can compete internationally, and now it is time to showcase this talent here in our own country. These leagues will offer role models to younger women and promote greater chances for female athletes, continuing the tradition of gender equity in sports. . . ." Confidence Builder: Humor Goes a Long Way Here are what I believe to be the top ten ways to be funny, taken from Wake 'Em Up!—How to Use Humor and Other Pro10 Days to More Confident Public Speaking 134 fessional Techniques to Create Alarmingly Good Business Presentations, by my colleague Tom Antion. 1. Anachronisms. An anachronism is a person, place, or thing that is out of its proper or chronological order. For instance, Paul Revere riding a motorcycle or George Washington sitting in front of a computer are humorous anachronisms. Any time you include an anachronistic relationship, you evoke humor and create more attention to your example, message, or point. Here's a good fill-in-the-blank format. Would [big name from the past] have —— if he had ——? All you have to do is make a simple relationship, and your message will be funny and memorable. For example: Would George Washington have thrown his money away in the Potomac if he had Fidelity Investment Management Associates on his side? 2. Audience gags. Audience gags are offbeat jokes that occur unexpectedly during a presentation. Dr. Joel Goodman developed this gag: A telephone rings during his presentation. He answers a phone that is hidden in the lectern and pretends to talk to his mother. The same joke would be called a “running gag” if the phone rang at several other times during the program. One of the more effective gags or skits I use in my program is the telephone exercise. In this exercise I choose two participants and have them sit in chairs with their backs to one another. I have one person pretend to call the other person with the objective of asking permission to send information. What the individual doesn’t know is that the person receiving the call has been instructed to not agree to anything without his or her boss’s permission. The person placing the call must use all possible sales and presentation techniques to 135 Language and Ethics convince the other person without getting angry. While this conversation is going on, I have the rest of the audience record the nonverbal expressions on each person’s face. When the conversation is concluded, the audience discusses the volunteer’s body language. The purpose of this exercise is to demonstrate that we use body language when we are on the phone even though the person we are speaking to cannot see us. The exercise also shows the audience how to remain professional, keep their cool, and gain a better understanding of how we use body language. 3. What is he talking about? One of Tom’s favorite gags is the false guest speaker. During this impersonation, Tom begins his presentation passing himself off as someone else. You can be as creative as you want with your impostor. He begins his speech pretending to know what he is talking about so it comes across as believable and authentic. He reveals his true identity only after he moves forward with his speech and starts to confuse the audience by talking about unrelated topics. Use this routine when you want to reduce audience pressure or just want to have some fun before you begin your speech. You can vary the length of the impostor’s speech to suit your program. 4. Cartoons. One of the most universally accepted forms of humor are cartoons. Here are three ways to use cartoons in your speeches: • Tell the audience about a cartoon you saw. • Cut out the cartoon from its publication and show it to your audience. Make sure you get permission before using it in your program. 10 Days to More Confident Public Speaking 136 • Make up a cartoon yourself. For example, when I give my speech “Overcoming Speaking Anxiety,” I use a cartoon depicting a speaker backed into a corner with a terrified look on his face. This cartoon represents how my clients sometimes feel trapped in a corner when they have to speak in front of a group. 5. Comic verse. Often a short poem illustrates your point better than hours of meaningless talking. Poems can be inspiring and motivating as well as funny. They also add variety to your presentations. You must flawlessly memorize any comic verse you use. Any stumble ruins the effect of the verse. If the verse is long, you may want to read it, but complete memorization has more impact. I don't usually use comic verse in my presentations; however, when I do use a comic verse, it's at the end of my presentation to leave the audience with something to remember. Sid Madwed, a very good friend and colleague of mine, is a professional poet and uses comic verse in many of his speeches. Here is an example of comic verse that Sid wrote about public speaking. I know someone who can talk a blue streak. Yet, if asked to speak in public says he'll freak. Is it any wonder that speaking in public is man's great fear? Ask a hundred to speak in public and none will volunteer. For most would feel funny and some will feel queer. But great power is yours if in public you speak with ease. For you can share what you know in a way that will please. For those who master speaking in public have the power of a Hercules. (Used with permission from Sid Madwed, www.madwed.com.) 137 Language and Ethics 6. Exaggeration. Expanding or diminishing proportions of your speech can be a fun way to create humor. It's similar to a caricature artist who outrageously exaggerates the features of an individual while still keeping the person recognizable. For example, Tom gave a talk for Secretary's Day at a large insurance company and focused on how hectic it always was for the secretaries. This is how he incorporated exaggeration into his presentation: "You're answering the telephone, the fax machine is ringing, you're making copies, and you're filing every policy clear back to 1910." The secretaries could relate to each item mentioned. They did a lot of filing, but certainly not as far back as 1910. Exaggerating this date lent humor while driving home the point that they always had lots of work piled up. 7. Fake facts and statistics. Stating falsehoods as if they were absolutely true is another fun way to play with the audience. However, you must make the statements obviously false by your words and your facial expressions. You don't want to leave any doubt about whether you are joking or being serious. For example, here is how Tom incorporated fake statistics into his presentation: "A study done for the Alaskan Pipeline Workers Union indicated that 97.2 percent of Alaskan Pipeline Workers wear panty hose." When giving fake statistics, use exact numbers for emphasis. 8. Roast humor. Being roasted (a tribute in which the honoree's friends and acquaintances alternate short speeches of praise and jokes) is a lot of fun, but you must be careful to honor the person you are roasting. Make jokes about things that are obviously untrue and 10 Days to More Confident Public Speaking 138 then exaggerate to make the humor even more obvious. Or you can outrageously exaggerate things about the individual that are true. Here is an example: "The emcee's job is not to be wise or witty. In fact, it is his job to appear dull so that the other speakers will shine in comparison. Considering who we are roasting tonight, it looks like I'm going to have to rise to new heights of boredom." 9. Quotations. Quotations are a safe bet to use: If they are not funny, you don't have to worry because you didn't write them. However, quotations can still be used to make your point. Thousands of notable quotations are available from quotation dictionaries, literature, and professional journals. Here are a few examples: "Get your facts first and then you can distort them as much as you please," by Mark Twain. "When you get to the end of your rope, tie a knot and hang on," by Franklin Delano Roosevelt. 10. Self-effacing humor. Self-effacing humor, or making fun of yourself, gets its strength from highlighting your own weaknesses. People who have the ability to laugh at themselves are perceived as secure, confident, strong, and likable. With this type of humor, a little goes a long way. If you overdo it, you will look like a doomsayer who is always putting yourself down. Seek out opportunities to tease yourself or make fun of your mistakes. This will be one of your most powerful tools to connect with the audience and a subtle way to show your strength. In my seminars I talk about the bad speaking habits I used to have and demonstrate a few by overexaggerating the gestures so that they look funny, but toned down enough so they're realistic. For example, I used to rise 139 Language and Ethics up and down on the balls of my feet. As I'm telling the audience about this behavior, I repeatedly rise up and down on the balls of my feet while swaying from side to side. The audience usually ends up laughing, and this tells them I'm not afraid to poke fun at myself. Type of Speech: Informative In Day 3 I discussed the different types of speeches: informative, demonstrative, persuasive, ceremonial, and impromptu or extemporaneous. Starting in this chapter and continuing through the remaining chapters of this book, I will give a portion of a sample speech so you can get a flavor of the different types of speeches and how to approach them. In this chapter I will share a portion of an informative speech. An informative speech gives the audience specific information about a certain topic or event. When I was still working as a nuclear materials engineer, I gave this speech—"Nuclear Power and How it Works"—to high school science classes studying nuclear power. Nuclear power is one of those things that keeps us in the light but so many of us are in the dark about it. Today, I am here to shed a little light on the subject and talk to you about nuclear power and how it works. To begin, let's take a look at how steam is created. Imagine a flask of water being heated by a flame and eventually you see the water begin to boil. After the water boils, it begins to generate steam, causing a whistling sound to come from the flask. The same result happens when you heat the flask with a hot plate. The only difference was the heat source, flame vs. hot plate. A nuclear power plant heats water the exact same way except the heat source is uranium dioxide, a special form of ura10 Days to More Confident Public Speaking 140 nium. When the uranium splits apart, it gives off heat and in turn heats the water to a boil. You may be asking why I selected a speech from my former career. As a professional speaker you are asked to make presentations on complicated, technical material. This speech worked well because I used simple terms and tried to explain the nuclear fission process using analogies and real-world examples that the students could relate to.

When you really get serious about improving your presentation and speaking skills, you will probably want professional coaching. A good speaking coach can objectively evaluate where you are now in your speaking abilities and help you formulate a plan to reach your goals. There are no quick fixes, but you can make significant improvement quickly, maybe in only a few weeks, if you work at it and have the proper direction. A speaking coach can evaluate you in person or with the help of a video or an audiotape. This tape is reviewed and an assessment is completed analyzing your strong points and what areas need improvement. If you are looking for a speaking coach, you can find a listing in the Yellow Pages or on the Internet. When you are talking with speaking coaches, whether on the phone or in person, be candid. Ask the coach for a list of clients he or she has worked with and testimonials from these clients. Ask how many years of experience the coach has in the field, if he or she has published any books, videos, or audiotapes. After gathering all the information, take time to review the facts and select a coach who will work best for you.

CHAPTER NINE

PAUSE AND POWER

The true business of the literary artist is to plait or weave his meaning, involving it around itself; so that each sentence, by successive phrases, shall first come into a kind of knot, and then, after a moment of suspended meaning, solve and clear itself. --GEORGE SAINTSBURY, on English Prose Style, in Miscellaneous Essays. ... pause ... has a distinctive value, expressed in silence; in other words, while the voice is waiting, the music of the movement is going on ... To manage it, with its delicacies and compensations, requires that same fineness of ear on which we must depend for all faultless prose rhythm. When there is no compensation, when the pause is inadvertent ... there is a sense of jolting and lack, as if some pin or fastening had fallen out. --JOHN FRANKLIN GENUNG, The Working Principles of Rhetoric. Pause, in public speech, is not mere silence--it is silence made designedly eloquent. When a man says: "I-uh-it is with profound-ah-pleasure that-er-I have been permitted to speak to you tonight and-uh-uh-I should say-er"--that is not pausing; that is stumbling. It is conceivable that a speaker may be effective in spite of stumbling--but never because of it. On the other hand, one of the most important means of developing power in public speaking is to pause either before or after, or both before and after, an important word or phrase. No one who would be a forceful speaker can afford to neglect this principle--one of the most significant that has ever been inferred from listening to great orators. Study this potential device until you have absorbed and assimilated it. It would seem that this principle of rhetorical pause ought to be easily grasped and applied, but a long experience in training both college men and maturer speakers has demonstrated that the device is no more readily understood by the average man when it is first explained to him than if it were spoken in Hindoostani. Perhaps this is because we do not eagerly devour the fruit of experience when it is impressively set before us on the platter of authority;

we like to pluck fruit for ourselves--it not only tastes better, but we never forget that tree! Fortunately, this is no difficult task, in this instance, for the trees stand thick all about us. One man is pleading the cause of another: "This man, my friends, has made this wonderful sacrifice--for you and me." Did not the pause surprisingly enhance the power of this statement? See how he gathered up reserve force and impressiveness to deliver the words "for you and me." Repeat this passage without making a pause. Did it lose in effectiveness? Naturally enough, during a premeditated pause of this kind the mind of the speaker is concentrated on the thought to which he is about to give expression. He will not dare to allow his thoughts to wander for an instant--he will rather supremely center his thought and his emotion upon the sacrifice whose service, sweetness and divinity he is enforcing by his appeal. Concentration, then, is the big word here--no pause without it can perfectly hit the mark. Efficient pausing accomplishes one or all of four results:

It is often dangerous to rush into battle without pausing for preparation or waiting for recruits. Consider Custer's massacre as an instance. You can light a match by holding it beneath a lens and concentrating the sun's rays. You would not expect the match to flame if you jerked the lens back and forth quickly. Pause, and the lens gathers the heat. Your thoughts will not set fire to the minds of your hearers unless you pause to gather the force that comes by a second or two of concentration. Maple trees and gas wells are rarely tapped continually; when a stronger flow is wanted, a pause is made, nature has time to gather her reserve forces, and when the tree or the well is reopened, a stronger flow is the result. Use the same common sense with your mind. If you would make a thought particularly effective, pause just before its utterance, concentrate your mind-energies, and then give it expression with renewed vigor. Carlyle was right: "Speak not, I passionately entreat thee, till thy thought has silently matured itself. Out of silence comes thy strength. Speech is silvern, Silence is golden; Speech is human, Silence is divine." Silence has been called the father of speech. It should be. Too many of our public speeches have no fathers. They ramble along without pause or break. Like Tennyson's brook, they run on forever. Listen to little children, the policeman on the corner, the family conversation around the table, and see how many pauses they naturally use, for they are unconscious of effects. When we get before an audience, we throw most of our natural methods of expression to the wind, and strive after artificial effects. Get back to the methods of nature--and pause. 2.

Pause Prepares the Mind of the Auditor to Receive Your Message Herbert Spencer said that all the universe is in motion. So it is--and all perfect motion is rhythm. Part of rhythm is rest. Rest follows activity all through nature. Instances: day and night; spring--summer--autumn--winter; a period of rest between breaths; an instant of complete rest between heart beats. Pause, and give the attention-powers of your audience a rest. What you say after such a silence will then have a great deal more effect. When your country cousins come to town, the noise of a passing car will awaken them, though it seldom affects a seasoned city dweller. By the continual passing of cars his attention-power has become deadened. In one who visits the city but seldom, attention-value is insistent. To him the noise comes after a long pause; hence its power. To you, dweller in the city, there is no pause; hence the low attention-value. After riding on a train several hours you will become so accustomed to its roar that it will lose its attention-value, unless the train should stop for a while and start again. If you attempt to listen to a clock-tick that is so far away that you can barely hear it, you will find that at times you are unable to distinguish it, but in a few moments the sound becomes distinct again. Your mind will pause for rest whether you desire it to do so or not. The attention of your audience will act in quite the same way. Recognize this law and prepare for it--by pausing. Let it be repeated: the thought that follows a pause is much more dynamic than if no pause had occurred. What is said to you of a night will not have the same effect on your mind as if it had been uttered in the morning when your attention had been lately refreshed by the pause of sleep. We are told on the first page of the Bible that even the Creative Energy of God rested on the "seventh day." You may be sure, then, that the frail finite mind of your audience will likewise demand rest. Observe nature, study her laws, and obey them in your speaking. 3. Pause Creates Effective Suspense Suspense is responsible for a great share of our interest in life; it will be the same with your speech. A play or CHAPTER VI 34 a novel is often robbed of much of its interest if you know the plot beforehand. We like to keep guessing as to the outcome. The ability to create suspense is part of woman's power to hold the other sex. The circus acrobat employs this principle when he fails purposely in several attempts to perform a feat, and then achieves it. Even the deliberate manner in which he arranges the preliminaries increases our expectation--we like to be kept waiting. In the last act of the play, "Polly of the Circus," there is a circus scene in which a little dog turns a backward somersault on the back of a running pony. One night when he hesitated and had to be coaxed and worked with a long time before he would perform his feat he got a great deal more applause than when he did his trick at once. We not only like to wait but we appreciate what we wait for. If fish bite too readily the sport soon ceases to be a sport. It is this same principle of suspense that holds you in a Sherlock Holmes story--you wait to see how the mystery is solved, and if it is solved too soon you throw down the tale unfinished. Wilkie Collins' receipt for fiction writing well applies to public speech: "Make 'em laugh; make 'em weep; make 'em wait." Above all else make them wait; if they will not do that you may be sure they will neither laugh nor weep. Thus pause is a valuable instrument in the hands of a trained speaker to arouse and maintain suspense. We once heard Mr. Bryan say in a speech: "It was my privilege to hear"--and he paused, while the audience wondered for a second whom it was his privilege to hear--"the great evangelist"--and he paused again; we knew a little more about the man he had heard, but still wondered to which evangelist he referred; and then he concluded: "Dwight L. Moody." Mr. Bryan paused slightly again and continued: "I came to regard him"--here he paused again and held the audience in a brief moment of suspense as to how he had regarded Mr. Moody, then continued--"as the greatest preacher of his day." Let the dashes illustrate pauses and we have the following: "It was my privilege to hear--the great evangelist--Dwight L. Moody.--I came to regard him--as the greatest preacher of his day." The unskilled speaker would have rattled this off with neither pause nor suspense, and the sentences would have fallen flat upon the audience. It is precisely the application of these small things that makes much of the difference between the successful and the unsuccessful speaker. 4. Pausing After An Important Idea Gives it Time to Penetrate Any Missouri farmer will tell you that a rain that falls too fast will run off into the creeks and do the crops but little good. A story is told of a country deacon praying for rain in this manner: "Lord, don't send us any chunk floater. Just give us a good old drizzle-drazzle." A speech, like a rain, will not do anybody much good if it comes too fast to soak in. The farmer's wife follows this same principle in doing her washing when she puts the clothes in water--and pauses for several hours that the water may soak in. The physician puts cocaine on your turbinates--and pauses to let it take hold before he removes them. Why do we use this principle everywhere except in the communication of ideas? If you have given the audience a big idea, pause for a second or two and let them turn it over. See what effect it has. After the smoke clears away you may have to fire another 14-inch shell on the same subject before you demolish the citadel of error that you are trying to destroy. Take time. Don't let your speech resemble those tourists who try "to do" New York in a day. They spend fifteen minutes looking at the masterpieces in the Metropolitan Museum of Arts, ten minutes in the Museum of Natural History, take a peep into the Aquarium, hurry across the Brooklyn Bridge, rush up to the Zoo, and back by Grant's Tomb--and call that "Seeing New York." If you hasten by your important points without pausing, your audience will have just about as adequate an idea of what you have tried to convey. Take time, you have just as much of it as our richest multimillionaire. Your audience will wait for you. It is a sign of smallness to hurry. The great redwood trees of California had burst through the soil five hundred years before Socrates drank his cup of hemlock poison, and are only in their prime today. Nature shames us with our petty haste. Silence is one of the most eloquent things in the world. Master it, and use it through pause.

In the following selections dashes have been inserted where pauses may be used effectively. Naturally, you may omit some of these and insert others without going wrong--one speaker would interpret a passage in one way, one in another; it is largely a matter of personal preference. A dozen great actors have played Hamlet well, and yet each has played the part differently. Which comes the nearest to perfection is a question of opinion. You will succeed best by daring to follow your own course--if you are individual enough to blaze an original trail. A moment's halt--a momentary taste of being from the well amid the waste--and lo! the phantom caravan has reached--the nothing it set out from--Oh make haste! The worldly hope men set their hearts upon--turns ashes--or it prospers;--and anon like snow upon the desert's dusty face--lighting a little hour or two--is gone. The bird of time has but a little way to flutter,--and the bird is on the wing. You will note that the punctuation marks have nothing to do with the pausing. You may run by a period very quickly and make a long pause where there is no kind of punctuation. Thought is greater than punctuation. It must guide you in your pauses. A book of verses underneath the bough,--a jug of wine, a loaf of bread--and thou beside me singing in the wilderness--Oh--wilderness were paradise enow. You must not confuse the pause for emphasis with the natural pauses that come through taking breath and phrasing. For example, note the pauses indicated in this selection from Byron: But hush!--hark!--that deep sound breaks in once more, And nearer!--clearer!--deadlier than before. Arm, ARM!--it is--it is the cannon's opening roar! It is not necessary to dwell at length upon these obvious distinctions. You will observe that in natural conversation our words are gathered into clusters or phrases, and we often pause to take breath between them. So in public speech, breathe naturally and do not talk until you must gasp for breath; nor until the audience is equally winded. A serious word of caution must here be uttered: do not overwork the pause. To do so will make your speech heavy and stilted. And do not think that pause can transmute commonplace thoughts into great and dignified utterance. A grand manner combined with insignificant ideas is like harnessing a Hambletonian with an ass. You remember the farcical old school declamation, "A Midnight Murder," that proceeded in grandiose manner to a thrilling climax, and ended--"and relentlessly murdered--a mosquito!" The pause, dramatically handled, always drew a laugh from the tolerant hearers. This is all very well in farce, but such anti-climax becomes painful when the speaker falls from the sublime to the ridiculous quite unintentionally. The pause, to be effective in some other manner than in that of the boomerang, must precede or follow a thought that is really worth while, or at least an idea whose bearing upon the rest of the speech is important. William Pittenger relates in his volume, "Extempore Speech," an instance of the unconsciously farcical use of the pause by a really great American statesman and orator. "He had visited Niagara Falls and was to make an oration at Buffalo the same day, but, unfortunately, he sat too long over the wine after dinner. When he arose to speak, the oratorical instinct struggled with difficulties, as he declared, 'Gentlemen, I have been to look upon your mag--mag--magnificent cataract, one hundred--and forty--seven--feet high! Gentlemen, Greece and CHAPTER VI 36 Rome in their palmiest days never had a cataract one hundred--and forty--seven--feet high!'"whisperings and the sweet vows of eternal love as they lingeringly part forever. Others are bending over cradles, kissing babies that are asleep. Some are receiving the blessings of old men. Some are parting from those who hold them and press them to their hearts again and again, and say nothing; and some are talking with wives, and endeavoring with brave words spoken in the old tones to drive from their hearts the awful fear. We see them part. We see the wife standing in the door, with the babe in her arms--standing in the sunlight sobbing; at the turn of the road a hand waves--she answers by holding high in her loving hands the child. He is gone--and forever. --ROBERT J. INGERSOLL, to the Soldiers of Indianapolis. 8. Where would you pause in the following selections? Try pausing in different places and note the effect it gives. The moving finger writes; and having writ moves on: nor all your piety nor wit shall lure it back to cancel half a line, nor all your tears wash out a word of it. The history of womankind is a story of abuse. For ages men beat, sold, and abused their wives and daughters like cattle. The Spartan mother that gave birth to one of her own sex disgraced herself; the girl babies were often deserted in the mountains to starve; China bound and deformed their feet; Turkey veiled their faces; America denied them equal educational advantages with men. Most of the world still refuses them the right to participate in the government and everywhere women bear the brunt of an unequal standard of morality. But the women are on the march. They are walking upward to the sunlit plains where the thinking people rule. China has ceased binding their feet. In the shadow of the Harem Turkey has opened a school for girls. America has given the women equal educational advantages, and America, we believe, will enfranchise them. We can do little to help and not much to hinder this great movement. The thinking people have put their O.K. upon it. It is moving forward to its goal just as surely as this old earth is swinging from the grip of winter toward the spring's blossoms and the summer's harvest.[1] 9. Read aloud the following address, paying careful attention to pause wherever the emphasis may thereby be heightened. THE IRREPRESSIBLE CONFLICT ... At last, the Republican party has appeared. It avows, now, as the Republican party of 1800 did, in one word, its faith and its works, "Equal and exact justice to all men." Even when it first entered the field, only half organized, it struck a blow which only just failed to secure complete and triumphant victory. In this, its second campaign, it has already won advantages which render that triumph now both easy and certain. The secret of its assured success lies in that very characteristic which, in the mouth of scoffers, constitutes its great and lasting imbecility and reproach. It lies in the fact that it is a party of one idea; but that is a noble one--an idea that fills and expands all generous souls; the idea of equality of all men before human tribunals and human laws, as they all are equal before the Divine tribunal and Divine laws. I know, and you know, that a revolution has begun. I know, and all the world knows, that revolutions never go backward. Twenty senators and a hundred representatives proclaim boldly in Congress to-day sentiments and opinions and principles of freedom which hardly so many men, even in this free State, dared to utter in their own homes twenty years ago. While the government of the United States, under the conduct of the Democratic party, has been all that time surrendering one plain and castle after another to slavery, the people of the United States have been no less steadily and perseveringly gathering together the forces with which to recover back again all the fields and all the castles which have been lost, and to confound and overthrow, by one decisive blow, the betrayers of the Constitution and freedom forever.

CHAPTER TEN

EFFICIENCY THROUGH INFLECTION

How soft the music of those village bells, Falling at intervals upon the ear In cadence sweet; now dying all away, Now pealing loud again, and louder still, Clear and sonorous, as the gale comes on! With easy force it opens all the cells Where Memory slept. --WILLIAM COWPER, The Task. Herbert Spencer remarked that "Cadence"--by which he meant the modulation of the tones of the voice in speaking--"is the running commentary of the emotions upon the propositions of the intellect." How true this is will appear when we reflect that the little upward and downward shadings of the voice tell more truly what we mean than our words. The expressiveness of language is literally multiplied by this subtle power to shade the vocal tones, and this voice-shading we call inflection. The change of pitch within a word is even more important, because more delicate, than the change of pitch from phrase to phrase. Indeed, one cannot be practised without the other. The bare words are only so many bricks--inflection will make of them a pavement, a garage, or a cathedral. It is the power of inflection to change the meaning of words that gave birth to the old saying: "It is not so much what you say, as how you say it." Mrs. Jameson, the Shakespearean commentator, has given us a penetrating example of the effect of inflection; "In her impersonation of the part of Lady Macbeth, Mrs. Siddons adopted successively three different intonations in giving the words 'We fail.' At first a quick contemptuous interrogation--'We fail?' Afterwards, with the note of admiration--'We fail,' an accent of indignant astonishment laying the principal emphasis on the word 'we'--'we fail.' Lastly, she fixed on what I am convinced is the true reading--We fail--with the simple period, modulating the voice to a deep, low, resolute tone which settles the issue at once as though she had said: 'If we fail, why then we fail, and all is over.'" This most expressive element of our speech is the last to be mastered in attaining to naturalness in speaking a foreign language, and its correct use is the main element in a natural, flexible utterance of our native tongue. Without varied inflections speech becomes wooden and monotonous. There are but two kinds of inflection, the rising and the falling, yet these two may be so shaded or so combined that they are capable of producing as many varieties of modulation as maybe illustrated by either one or two lines, straight or curved, thus: [Illustration of each line] Sharp rising Long rising Level Long falling Sharp falling Sharp rising and falling CHAPTER VII 40 Sharp falling and rising Hesitating These may be varied indefinitely, and serve merely to illustrate what wide varieties of combination may be effected by these two simple inflections of the voice. It is impossible to tabulate the various inflections which serve to express various shades of thought and feeling. A few suggestions are offered here, together with abundant exercises for practise, but the only real way to master inflection is to observe, experiment, and practise. For example, take the common sentence, "Oh, he's all right." Note how a rising inflection may be made to express faint praise, or polite doubt, or uncertainty of opinion. Then note how the same words, spoken with a generally falling inflection may denote certainty, or good-natured approval, or enthusiastic praise, and so on. In general, then, we find that a bending upward of the voice will suggest doubt and uncertainty, while a decided falling inflection will suggest that you are certain of your ground. Students dislike to be told that their speeches are "not so bad," spoken with a rising inflection. To enunciate these words with a long falling inflection would indorse the speech rather heartily. Say good-bye to an imaginary person whom you expect to see again tomorrow; then to a dear friend you never expect to meet again. Note the difference in inflection. "I have had a delightful time," when spoken at the termination of a formal tea by a frivolous woman takes altogether different inflection than the same words spoken between lovers who have enjoyed themselves. Mimic the two characters in repeating this and observe the difference. Note how light and short the inflections are in the following brief quotation from "Anthony the Absolute," by Samuel Mervin. At Sea--March 28th. This evening I told Sir Robert What's His Name he was a fool. I was quite right in this. He is. Every evening since the ship left Vancouver he has presided over the round table in the middle of the smoking-room. There he sips his coffee and liqueur, and holds forth on every subject known to the mind of man. Each subject is his subject. He is an elderly person, with a bad face and a drooping left eyelid. They tell me that he is in the British Service--a judge somewhere down in Malaysia, where they drink more than is good for them. Deliver the two following selections with great earnestness, and note how the inflections differ from the foregoing. Then reread these selections in a light, superficial manner, noting that the change of attitude is expressed through a change of inflection. When I read a sublime fact in Plutarch, or an unselfish deed in a line of poetry, or thrill beneath some heroic legend, it is no longer fairyland--I have seen it matched. --WENDELL PHILLIPS. CHAPTER VII 41 Thought is deeper than all speech, Feeling deeper than all thought; Souls to souls can never teach What unto themselves was taught. --CRANCH It must be made perfectly clear that inflection deals mostly in subtle, delicate shading within single words, and is not by any means accomplished by a general rise or fall in the voice in speaking a sentence. Yet certain sentences may be effectively delivered with just such inflection. Try this sentence in several ways, making no modulation until you come to the last two syllables, as indicated,Now try this sentence by inflecting the important words so as to bring out various shades of meaning. The first forms, illustrated above, show change of pitch within a single word; the forms you will work out for yourself should show a number of such inflections throughout the sentence. One of the chief means of securing emphasis is to employ a long falling inflection on the emphatic words--that is, to let the voice fall to a lower pitch on an interior vowel sound in a word. Try it on the words "every," "eleemosynary," and "destroy." Use long falling inflections on the italicized words in the following selection, noting their emphatic power. Are there any other words here that long falling inflections would help to make expressive? ADDRESS IN THE DARTMOUTH COLLEGE CASE This, sir, is my case. It is the case not merely of that humble institution; it is the case of every college in our land. It is more; it is the case of every eleemosynary institution throughout our country--of all those great charities founded by the piety of our ancestors to alleviate human misery and scatter blessings along the pathway of life. Sir, you may destroy this little institution--it is weak, it is in your hands. I know it is one of the lesser lights in the literary horizon of our country. You may put it out. But if you do you must carry through your work; you must extinguish, one after another, all those great lights of science which, for more than a century, have thrown their radiance over our land! It is, sir, as I have said, a small college, and yet--there are those who love it! Sir, I know not how others may feel, but as for myself when I see my alma mater surrounded, like Cæsar in the senate house, by those who are reiterating stab after stab, I would not for this right hand have her turn to me and say, And thou, too, my son! --DANIEL WEBSTER. Be careful not to over-inflect. Too much modulation produces an unpleasant effect of artificiality, like a mature matron trying to be kittenish. It is a short step between true expression and unintentional burlesque. Scrutinize your own tones. Take a single expression like "Oh, no!" or "Oh, I see," or "Indeed," and by patient self-examination see how many shades of meaning may be expressed by inflection. This sort of common-sense practise will do you more good than a book of rules. But don't forget to listen to your own voice. QUESTIONS AND EXERCISES 1. In your own words define (a) cadence, (b) modulation, (c) inflection, (d) emphasis. CHAPTER VII 42 2. Name five ways of destroying monotony and gaining effectiveness in speech. 3. What states of mind does falling inflection signify? Make as full a list as you can. 4. Do the same for the rising inflection. 5. How does the voice bend in expressing (a) surprise? (b) shame? (c) hate? (d) formality? (e) excitement? 6. Reread some sentence several times and by using different inflections change the meaning with each reading. 7. Note the inflections employed in some speech or conversation. Were they the best that could be used to bring out the meaning? Criticise and illustrate. 8. Render the following passages: Has the gentleman done? Has he completely done? And God said, Let there be light: and there was light. 9. Invent an indirect question and show how it would naturally be inflected. 10. Does a direct question always require a rising inflection? Illustrate. 11. Illustrate how the complete ending of an expression or of a speech is indicated by inflection. 12. Do the same for incompleteness of idea. 13. Illustrate (a) trembling, (b) hesitation, and (c) doubt by means of inflection. 14. Show how contrast may be expressed. 15. Try the effects of both rising and falling inflections on the italicized words in the following sentences. State your preference. Gentlemen, I am persuaded, nay, I am resolved to speak. It is sown a natural body; it is raised a spiritual body. SELECTIONS FOR PRACTISE In the following selections secure emphasis by means of long falling inflections rather than loudness. Repeat these selections, attempting to put into practise all the technical principles that we have thus far had; emphasizing important words, subordinating unimportant words, variety of pitch, changing tempo, pause, and inflection. If these principles are applied you will have no trouble with monotony. Constant practise will give great facility in the use of inflection and will render the voice itself flexible.

CHARLES I We charge him with having broken his coronation oath; and we are told that he kept his marriage vow! We CHAPTER VII 43 accuse him of having given up his people to the merciless inflictions of the most hot-headed and hard-hearted of prelates; and the defence is, that he took his little son on his knee and kissed him! We censure him for having violated the articles of the Petition of Right, after having, for good and valuable consideration, promised to observe them; and we are informed that he was accustomed to hear prayers at six o'clock in the morning! It is to such considerations as these, together with his Vandyke dress, his handsome face, and his peaked beard, that he owes, we verily believe, most of his popularity with the present generation. --T.B. MACAULAY. ABRAHAM LINCOLN We needed not that he should put on paper that he believed in slavery, who, with treason, with murder, with cruelty infernal, hovered around that majestic man to destroy his life. He was himself but the long sting with which slavery struck at liberty; and he carried the poison that belonged to slavery. As long as this nation lasts, it will never be forgotten that we have one martyred President--never! Never, while time lasts, while heaven lasts, while hell rocks and groans, will it be forgotten that slavery, by its minions, slew him, and in slaying him made manifest its whole nature and tendency. But another thing for us to remember is that this blow was aimed at the life of the government and of the nation. Lincoln was slain; America was meant. The man was cast down; the government was smitten at. It was the President who was killed. It was national life, breathing freedom and meaning beneficence, that was sought. He, the man of Illinois, the private man, divested of robes and the insignia of authority, representing nothing but his personal self, might have been hated; but that would not have called forth the murderer's blow. It was because he stood in the place of government, representing government and a government that represented right and liberty, that he was singled out. This, then, is a crime against universal government. It is not a blow at the foundations of our government, more than at the foundations of the English government, of the French government, of every compact and well-organized government. It was a crime against mankind. The whole world will repudiate and stigmatize it as a deed without a shade of redeeming light.... The blow, however, has signally failed. The cause is not stricken; it is strengthened. This nation has dissolved,--but in tears only. It stands, four-square, more solid, to-day, than any pyramid in Egypt. This people are neither wasted, nor daunted, nor disordered. Men hate slavery and love liberty with stronger hate and love to-day than ever before. The Government is not weakened, it is made stronger.... And now the martyr is moving in triumphal march, mightier than when alive. The nation rises up at every stage of his coming. Cities and states are his pall-bearers, and the cannon beats the hours with solemn progression. Dead--dead--dead--he yet speaketh! Is Washington dead? Is Hampden dead? Is David dead? Is any man dead that ever was fit to live? Disenthralled of flesh, and risen to the unobstructed sphere where passion never comes, he begins his illimitable work. His life now is grafted upon the Infinite, and will be fruitful as no earthly life can be. Pass on, thou that hast overcome! Your sorrows O people, are his peace! Your bells, and bands, and muffled drums sound triumph in his ear. Wail and weep here; God makes it echo joy and triumph there. Pass on, victor! Four years ago, O Illinois, we took from your midst an untried man, and from among the people; we return him to you a mighty conqueror. Not thine any more, but the nation's; not ours, but the world's. Give him place, ye prairies! In the midst of this great Continent his dust shall rest, a sacred treasure to myriads who shall make pilgrimage to that shrine to kindle anew their zeal and patriotism. Ye winds, that move over the mighty places of the West, chant his requiem! Ye people, behold a martyr, whose blood, as so many inarticulate words, pleads for fidelity, for law, for liberty!The event which we commemorate is all-important, not merely in our own annals, but in those of the world. The sententious English poet has declared that "the proper study of mankind is man," and of all inquiries of a temporal nature, the history of our fellow-beings is unquestionably among the most interesting. But not all the chapters of human history are alike important. The annals of our race have been filled up with incidents which concern not, or at least ought not to concern, the great company of mankind. History, as it has often been written, is the genealogy of princes, the field-book of conquerors; and the fortunes of our fellow-men have been treated only so far as they have been affected by the influence of the great masters and destroyers of our race. Such history is, I will not say a worthless study, for it is necessary for us to know the dark side as well as the bright side of our condition. But it is a melancholy study which fills the bosom of the philanthropist and the friend of liberty with sorrow. But the history of liberty--the history of men struggling to be free--the history of men who have acquired and are exercising their freedom--the history of those great movements in the world, by which liberty has been established and perpetuated, forms a subject which we cannot contemplate too closely.

This is the real history of man, of the human family, of rational immortal beings.... The trial of adversity was theirs; the trial of prosperity is ours. Let us meet it as men who know their duty and prize their blessings. Our position is the most enviable, the most responsible, which men can fill. If this generation does its duty, the cause of constitutional freedom is safe. If we fail--if we fail--not only do we defraud our children of the inheritance which we received from our fathers, but we blast the hopes of the friends of liberty throughout our continent, throughout Europe, throughout the world, to the end of time. History is not without her examples of hard-fought fields, where the banner of liberty has floated triumphantly on the wildest storm of battle. She is without her examples of a people by whom the dear-bought treasure has been wisely employed and safely handed down. The eyes of the world are turned for that example to us.... Let us, then, as we assemble on the birthday of the nation, as we gather upon the green turf, once wet with precious blood--let us devote ourselves to the sacred cause of constitutional liberty! Let us abjure the interests and passions which divide the great family of American freemen! Let the rage of party spirit sleep to-day! Let us resolve that our children shall have cause to bless the memory of their fathers, as we have cause to bless the memory of ours!CONCENTRATION IN DELIVERY Attention is the microscope of the mental eye. Its power may be high or low; its field of view narrow or broad. When high power is used attention is confined within very circumscribed limits, but its action is exceedingly intense and absorbing. It sees but few things, but these few are observed "through and through" ... Mental energy and activity, whether of perception or of thought, thus concentrated, act like the sun's rays concentrated by the burning glass. The object is illumined, heated, set on fire. Impressions are so deep that they can never be effaced. Attention of this sort is the prime condition of the most productive mental labor. --DANIEL PUTNAM, Psychology. Try to rub the top of your head forward and backward at the same time that you are patting your chest. Unless your powers of coördination are well developed you will find it confusing, if not impossible. The brain needs special training before it can do two or more things efficiently at the same instant. It may seem like splitting a hair between its north and northwest corner, but some psychologists argue that no brain can think two distinct thoughts, absolutely simultaneously--that what seems to be simultaneous is really very rapid rotation from the first thought to the second and back again, just as in the above-cited experiment the attention must shift from one hand to the other until one or the other movement becomes partly or wholly automatic. Whatever is the psychological truth of this contention it is undeniable that the mind measurably loses grip on one idea the moment the attention is projected decidedly ahead to a second or a third idea. A fault in public speakers that is as pernicious as it is common is that they try to think of the succeeding sentence while still uttering the former, and in this way their concentration trails off; in consequence, they start their sentences strongly and end them weakly. In a well-prepared written speech the emphatic word usually comes at one end of the sentence. But an emphatic word needs emphatic expression, and this is precisely what it does not get when concentration flags by leaping too soon to that which is next to be uttered. Concentrate all your mental energies on the present sentence. Remember that the mind of your audience follows yours very closely, and if you withdraw your attention from what you are saying to what you are going to say, your audience will also withdraw theirs. They may not do so consciously and deliberately, but they will surely cease to give importance to the things that you yourself slight. It is fatal to either the actor or the speaker to cross his bridges too soon. Of course, all this is not to say that in the natural pauses of your speech you are not to take swift forward surveys--they are as important as the forward look in driving a motor car; the caution is of quite another sort: while speaking one sentence do not think of the sentence to follow. Let it come from its proper source--within yourself. You cannot deliver a broadside without concentrated force--that is what produces the explosion. In preparation you store and concentrate thought and feeling; in the pauses during delivery you swiftly look ahead and gather yourself for effective attack; during the moments of actual speech, SPEAK--DON'T ANTICIPATE. Divide your attention and you divide your power. This matter of the effect of the inner man upon the outer needs a further word here, particularly as touching concentration. "What do you read, my lord?" Hamlet replied, "Words. Words. Words." That is a world-old trouble. The mechanical calling of words is not expression, by a long stretch. Did you ever notice how hollow a memorized speech usually sounds? You have listened to the ranting, mechanical cadence of inefficient actors, lawyers and preachers. Their trouble is a mental one--they are not concentratedly thinking thoughts that cause words to issue with sincerity and conviction, but are merely enunciating word-sounds mechanically. Painful CHAPTER VIII 46 experience alike to audience and to speaker! A parrot is equally eloquent. Again let Shakespeare instruct us, this tune in the insincere prayer of the King, Hamlet's uncle. He laments thus pointedly: My words fly up, my thoughts remain below: Words without thoughts never to heaven go. The truth is, that as a speaker your words must be born again every time they are spoken, then they will not suffer in their utterance, even though perforce committed to memory and repeated, like Dr. Russell Conwell's lecture, "Acres of Diamonds," five thousand times. Such speeches lose nothing by repetition for the perfectly patent reason that they arise from concentrated thought and feeling and not a mere necessity for saying something--which usually means anything, and that, in turn, is tantamount to nothing. If the thought beneath your words is warm, fresh, spontaneous, a part of your self, your utterance will have breath and life. Words are only a result. Do not try to get the result without stimulating the cause. Do you ask how to concentrate? Think of the word itself, and of its philological brother, concentric. Think of how a lens gathers and concenters the rays of light within a given circle. It centers them by a process of withdrawal. It may seem like a harsh saying, but the man who cannot concentrate is either weak of will, a nervous wreck, or has never learned what will-power is good for. You must concentrate by resolutely withdrawing your attention from everything else. If you concentrate your thought on a pain which may be afflicting you, that pain will grow more intense. "Count your blessings" and they will multiply. Center your thought on your strokes and your tennis play will gradually improve. To concentrate is simply to attend to one thing, and attend to nothing else. If you find that you cannot do that, there is something wrong--attend to that first. Remove the cause and the symptom will disappear. Read the chapter on "Will Power." Cultivate your will by willing and then doing, at all costs. Concentrate--and you will win. QUESTIONS AND EXERCISES 1. Select from any source several sentences suitable for speaking aloud; deliver them first in the manner condemned in this chapter, and second with due regard for emphasis toward the close of each sentence. 2. Put into about one hundred words your impression of the effect produced. 3. Tell of any peculiar methods you may have observed or heard of by which speakers have sought to aid their powers of concentration, such as looking fixedly at a blank spot in the ceiling, or twisting a watch charm. 4. What effect do such habits have on the audience? 5. What relation does pause bear to concentration? 6. Tell why concentration naturally helps a speaker to change pitch, tempo, and emphasis. 7. Read the following selection through to get its meaning and spirit clearly in your mind. Then read it aloud, concentrating solely on the thought that you are expressing--do not trouble about the sentence or thought that is coming. Half the troubles of mankind arise from anticipating trials that never occur. Avoid this in speaking. Make the end of your sentences just as strong as the beginning. CONCENTRATE. WAR! The last of the savage instincts is war. The cave man's club made law and procured food. Might decreed right. Warriors were saviours. CHAPTER VIII 47 In Nazareth a carpenter laid down the saw and preached the brotherhood of man. Twelve centuries afterwards his followers marched to the Holy Land to destroy all who differed with them in the worship of the God of Love. Triumphantly they wrote "In Solomon's Porch and in his temple our men rode in the blood of the Saracens up to the knees of their horses." History is an appalling tale of war. In the seventeenth century Germany, France, Sweden, and Spain warred for thirty years. At Magdeburg 30,000 out of 36,000 were killed regardless of sex or age. In Germany schools were closed for a third of a century, homes burned, women outraged, towns demolished, and the untilled land became a wilderness. Two-thirds of Germany's property was destroyed and 18,000,000 of her citizens were killed, because men quarrelled about the way to glorify "The Prince of Peace." Marching through rain and snow, sleeping on the ground, eating stale food or starving, contracting diseases and facing guns that fire six hundred times a minute, for fifty cents a day--this is the soldier's life. At the window sits the widowed mother crying. Little children with tearful faces pressed against the pane watch and wait. Their means of livelihood, their home, their happiness is gone. Fatherless children, broken-hearted women, sick, disabled and dead men--this is the wage of war. We spend more money preparing men to kill each other than we do in teaching them to live. We spend more money building one battleship than in the annual maintenance of all our state universities. The financial loss resulting from destroying one another's homes in the civil war would have built 15,000,000 houses, each costing $2,000. We pray for love but prepare for hate. We preach peace but equip for war. Were half the power that fills the world with terror, Were half the wealth bestowed on camp and court Given to redeem this world from error, There would be no need of arsenal and fort. War only defers a question. No issue will ever really be settled until it is settled rightly. Like rival "gun gangs" in a back alley, the nations of the world, through the bloody ages, have fought over their differences. Denver cannot fight Chicago and Iowa cannot fight Ohio. Why should Germany be permitted to fight France, or Bulgaria fight Turkey? When mankind rises above creeds, colors and countries, when we are citizens, not of a nation, but of the world, the armies and navies of the earth will constitute an international police force to preserve the peace and the dove will take the eagle's place. Our differences will be settled by an international court with the power to enforce its mandates. In times of peace prepare for peace. The wages of war are the wages of sin, and the "wages of sin is death."You have attended plays that seemed fair, yet they did not move you, grip you. In theatrical parlance, they failed to "get over," which means that their message did not get over the foot-lights to the audience. There was no punch, no jab to them--they had no force. Of course, all this spells disaster, in big letters, not only in a stage production but in any platform effort. Every such presentation exists solely for the audience, and if it fails to hit them--and the expression is a good one--it has no excuse for living; nor will it live long. What is Force? Some of our most obvious words open up secret meanings under scrutiny, and this is one of them. To begin with, we must recognize the distinction between inner and outer force. The one is cause, the other effect. The one is spiritual, the other physical. In this important particular, animate force differs from inanimate force--the power of man, coming from within and expressing itself outwardly, is of another sort from the force of Shimose powder, which awaits some influence from without to explode it. However susceptive to outside stimuli, the true source of power in man lies within himself. This may seem like "mere psychology," but it has an intensely practical bearing on public speaking, as will appear. Not only must we discern the difference between human force and mere physical force, but we must not confuse its real essence with some of the things that may--and may not--accompany it. For example, loudness is not force, though force at times may be attended by noise. Mere roaring never made a good speech, yet there are moments--moments, mind you, not minutes--when big voice power may be used with tremendous effect. Nor is violent motion force--yet force may result in violent motion. Hamlet counseled the players: Nor do not saw the air too much with your hand, thus; but use all gently; for in the very torrent, tempest, and (as I may say) whirlwind of your passion, you must acquire and beget a temperance, that may give it smoothness. Oh, it offends me to the soul, to hear a robustious periwig-pated fellow tear a passion to tatters, to very rags, to split the ears of the groundlings[2]; who, for the most part, are capable of nothing but inexplicable dumb show, and noise. I would have such a fellow whipped for o'er-doing Termagant; it out-herods Herod. Pray you avoid it. Be not too tame, neither, but let your discretion be your tutor: suit the action to the word, the word to the action; with this special observance, that you o'erstep not the modesty of nature; for anything so overdone is from the purpose of playing, whose end, both at the first, and now, was, and is, to hold, as 'twere, the mirror up to Nature, to show Virtue her own feature, Scorn her own image, and the very age and body of the time his form and pressure. Now, this overdone, or come tardy off, though it make the unskillful laugh, cannot but make the judicious grieve; the censure of the which one must, in your allowance, o'erweigh a whole theater of others. Oh, there be players that I have seen play--and heard others praise, and that highly--not to speak it profanely, that, neither having the accent of Christians, nor the gait of Christian, pagan, or man, have so strutted and bellowed that I have thought some of Nature's journeymen had made men, and not made them CHAPTER IX 49 well, they imitated humanity so abominably.[3] Force is both a cause and an effect. Inner force, which must precede outer force, is a combination of four elements, acting progressively. First of all, force arises from conviction. You must be convinced of the truth, or the importance, or the meaning, of what you are about to say before you can give it forceful delivery. It must lay strong hold upon your convictions before it can grip your audience. Conviction convinces. The Saturday Evening Post in an article on "England's T.R."--Winston Spencer Churchill--attributed much of Churchill's and Roosevelt's public platform success to their forceful delivery. No matter what is in hand, these men make themselves believe for the time being that that one thing is the most important on earth. Hence they speak to their audiences in a Do-this-or-you-PERISH manner. That kind of speaking wins, and it is that virile, strenuous, aggressive attitude which both distinguishes and maintains the platform careers of our greatest leaders. But let us look a little closer at the origins of inner force. How does conviction affect the man who feels it? We have answered the inquiry in the very question itself--he feels it: Conviction produces emotional tension. Study the pictures of Theodore Roosevelt and of Billy Sunday in action--action is the word. Note the tension of their jaw muscles, the taut lines of sinews in their entire bodies when reaching a climax of force. Moral and physical force are alike in being both preceded and accompanied by in-tens-ity--tension--tightness of the cords of power. It is this tautness of the bow-string, this knotting of the muscles, this contraction before the spring, that makes an audience feel--almost see--the reserve power in a speaker. In some really wonderful way it is more what a speaker does not say and do that reveals the dynamo within. Anything may come from such stored-up force once it is let loose; and that keeps an audience alert, hanging on the lips of a speaker for his next word. After all, it is all a question of manhood, for a stuffed doll has neither convictions nor emotional tension. If you are upholstered with sawdust, keep off the platform, for your own speech will puncture you. Growing out of this conviction-tension comes resolve to make the audience share that conviction-tension. Purpose is the backbone of force; without it speech is flabby--it may glitter, but it is the iridescence of the spineless jellyfish. You must hold fast to your resolve if you would hold fast to your audience. Finally, all this conviction-tension-purpose is lifeless and useless unless it results in propulsion. You remember how Young in his wonderful "Night Thoughts" delineates the man who Pushes his prudent purpose to resolve, Resolves, and re-resolves, and dies the same. Let not your force "die a-borning,"--bring it to full life in its conviction, emotional tension, resolve, and propulsive power. Can Force be Acquired? Yes, if the acquirer has any such capacities as we have just outlined. How to acquire this vital factor is suggested in its very analysis: Live with your subject until you are convinced of its importance. If your message does not of itself arouse you to tension, PULLyourself together. When a man faces the necessity of leaping across a crevasse he does not wait for inspiration, he wills his muscles into tensity for the spring--it is not without purpose that our English language uses the same word to depict a mighty though delicate steel contrivance and a quick leap through the air. Then resolve--and let it all end in actual punch. This truth is worth reiteration: The man within is the final factor. He must supply the fuel. The audience, or CHAPTER IX 50 even the man himself, may add the match--it matters little which, only so that there be fire. However skillfully your engine is constructed, however well it works, you will have no force if the fire has gone out under the boiler. It matters little how well you have mastered poise, pause, modulation, and tempo, if your speech lacks fire it is dead. Neither a dead engine nor a dead speech will move anybody. Four factors of force are measurably within your control, and in that far may be acquired: ideas, feeling about the subject, wording, and delivery. Each of these is more or less fully discussed in this volume, except wording, which really requires a fuller rhetorical study than can here be ventured. It is, however, of the utmost importance that you should be aware of precisely how wording bears upon force in a sentence. Study "The Working Principles of Rhetoric," by John Franklin Genung, or the rhetorical treatises of Adams Sherman

Hill, of Charles Sears Baldwin, or any others whose names may easily be learned from any teacher. Here are a few suggestions on the use of words to attain force: Choice of Words PLAIN words are more forceful than words less commonly used--jugglehas more vigor than prestidigitate. SHORT words are stronger than long words--end has more directness than terminate. SAXON words are usually more forceful than Latinistic words--for force, use wars against rather than militate against. SPECIFIC words are stronger than general words--pressman is more definite than printer. CONNOTATIVE words, those that suggest more than they say, have more power than ordinary words--"She let herself be married" expresses more than "She married." EPITHETS, figuratively descriptive words, are more effective than direct names--"Go tell that old fox," has more "punch" than "Go tell that sly fellow." ONOMATOPOETIC words, words that convey the sense by the sound, are more powerful than other words--crash is more effective than cataclysm. Arrangement of words Cut out modifiers. Cut out connectives. Begin with words that demand attention. "End with words that deserve distinction," says Prof. Barrett Wendell. Set strong ideas over against weaker ones, so as to gain strength by the contrast. Avoid elaborate sentence structure--short sentences are stronger than long ones. Cut out every useless word, so as to give prominence to the really important ones. Let each sentence be a condensed battering ram, swinging to its final blow on the attention. A familiar, homely idiom, if not worn by much use, is more effective than a highly formal, scholarly expression. CHAPTER IX 51 Consider well the relative value of different positions in the sentence so that you may give the prominent place to ideas you wish to emphasize. "But," says someone, "is it not more honest to depend the inherent interest in a subject, its native truth, clearness and sincerity of presentation, and beauty of utterance, to win your audience? Why not charm men instead of capturing them by assault?" Why Use Force? There is much truth in such an appeal, but not all the truth. Clearness, persuasion, beauty, simple statement of truth, are all essential--indeed, they are all definite parts of a forceful presentment of a subject, without being the only parts. Strong meat may not be as attractive as ices, but all depends on the appetite and the stage of the meal. You can not deliver an aggressive message with caressing little strokes. No! Jab it in with hard, swift solar plexus punches. You cannot strike fire from flint or from an audience with love taps. Say to a crowded theatre in a lackadaisical manner: "It seems to me that the house is on fire," and your announcement may be greeted with a laugh. If you flash out the words: "The house's on fire!" they will crush one another in getting to the exits. The spirit and the language of force are definite with conviction. No immortal speech in literature contains such expressions as "it seems to me," "I should judge," "in my opinion," "I suppose," "perhaps it is true." The speeches that will live have been delivered by men ablaze with the courage of their convictions, who uttered their words as eternal truth. Of Jesus it was said that "the common people heard Him gladly." Why? "He taught them as one having AUTHORITY." An audience will never be moved by what "seems" to you to be truth or what in your "humble opinion" may be so. If you honestly can, assert convictions as your conclusions. Be sure you are right before you speak your speech, then utter your thoughts as though they were a Gibraltar of unimpeachable truth. Deliver them with the iron hand and confidence of a Cromwell. Assert them with the fire of authority. Pronounce them as an ultimatum. If you cannot speak with conviction, be silent. What force did that young minister have who, fearing to be too dogmatic, thus exhorted his hearers: "My friends--as I assume that you are--it appears to be my duty to tell you that if you do not repent, so to speak, forsake your sins, as it were, and turn to righteousness, if I may so express it, you will be lost, in a measure"? Effective speech must reflect the era. This is not a rose water age, and a tepid, half-hearted speech will not win. This is the century of trip hammers, of overland expresses that dash under cities and through mountain tunnels, and you must instill this spirit into your speech if you would move a popular audience. From a front seat listen to a first-class company present a modern Broadway drama--not a comedy, but a gripping, thrilling drama. Do not become absorbed in the story; reserve all your attention for the technique and the force of the acting. There is a kick and a crash as well as an infinitely subtle intensity in the big, climax-speeches that suggest this lesson: the same well-calculated, restrained, delicately shaded force would simply rivet your ideas in the minds of your audience. An air-gun will rattle bird-shot against a window pane--it takes a rifle to wing a bullet through plate glass and the oaken walls beyond. When to Use Force An audience is unlike the kingdom of heaven--the violent do not always take it by force. There are times when beauty and serenity should be the only bells in your chime. Force is only one of the great extremes of contrast--use neither it nor quiet utterance to the exclusion of other tones: be various, and in variety find even greater force than you could attain by attempting its constant use. If you are reading an essay on the beauties of the dawn, talking about the dainty bloom of a honey-suckle, or explaining the mechanism of a gas engine, a vigorous style of delivery is entirely out of place. But when you are appealing to wills and consciences for CHAPTER IX 52 immediate action, forceful delivery wins. In such cases, consider the minds of your audience as so many safes that have been locked and the keys lost. Do not try to figure out the combinations. Pour a little nitro glycerine into the cracks and light the fuse. As these lines are being written a contractor down the street is clearing away the rocks with dynamite to lay the foundations for a great building. When you want to get action, do not fear to use dynamite. The final argument for the effectiveness of force in public speech is the fact that everything must be enlarged for the purposes of the platform--that is why so few speeches read well in the reports on the morning after: statements appear crude and exaggerated because they are unaccompanied by the forceful delivery of a glowing speaker before an audience heated to attentive enthusiasm. So in preparing your speech you must not err on the side of mild statement--your audience will inevitably tone down your words in the cold grey of afterthought. When Phidias was criticised for the rough, bold outlines of a figure he had submitted in competition, he smiled and asked that his statue and the one wrought by his rival should be set upon the column for which the sculpture was destined. When this was done all the exaggerations and crudities, toned by distances, melted into exquisite grace of line and form. Each speech must be a special study in suitability and proportion. Omit the thunder of delivery, if you will, but like Wendell Phillips put "silent lightning" into your speech. Make your thoughts breathe and your words burn. Birrell said: "Emerson writes like an electrical cat emitting sparks and shocks in every sentence." Go thou and speak likewise. Get the "big stick" into your delivery--be forceful.

CHAPTER ELEVEN

Expect the Unexpected

There comes a time when you have put your heart and soul into preparing your presentation. You have spent hours, if not days, making sure you have reviewed all your notes, visual aids, and gestures and verified that the room in which you will be giving your presentation is reserved. However, when you arrive at the location, you find that something is wrong with the room, the equipment, or both. Preparing for the unexpected, such as your slides falling in a puddle or drawing a complete blank just as you step up to the lectern, is the focus of this chapter. I will provide you with tips and ad libs to use when you find yourself in deep trouble. Furthermore, I will share secrets that professional speakers, trainers, and entertainers use to get themselves out of a jam. These ideas and suggestions will work only if you plan for them beforehand and practice how to handle them. The more you anticipate problems ahead of time, the better prepared you are if they should happen. And believe me, there will come a time when something will creep up on you before or during your presentation. Worrying about these situations leads to speaking anxiety, nervousness, and a lack of self-confidence; however, if you ac- cept the fact that problems happen, you can better prepare yourself for the unexpected. How to Prepare for the Unexpected Novice public speakers believe that their presentation needs to be perfect or the audience will not respect them. This belief couldn't be further from the truth. Audiences, by nature, want you to succeed and are willing to help make it happen. Let's look at some classic problems that many speakers (including myself) have experienced, such as problems with microphones, PA systems, overhead projectors, slide projectors, or the dais itself. In addition, I will discuss real-life situations that have occurred for many professional speakers and offer solutions to prevent, or at least minimize, these problems. Microphone Problems Today speakers use several different types of microphones, and each takes practice to learn how to use properly. For instance, holding a microphone in your hand while speaking is different from speaking into a microphone attached to the lectern. • Problem number 1. The microphone goes dead in the middle of your presentation. Solution. In the event your microphone goes dead in the middle of your presentation, and you don't have a spare, turn off the microphone. Apologize to the audience. Then walk out to where the audience is sitting so they can hear you and make sure you project your voice to the back of the room. When you reach a 10 Days to More Confident Public Speaking 144 breaking point in your speech, stop and see if you can locate another microphone. • Problem number 2. Distortion problems. This includes problems such as popping noises—sounds caused by your mouth when you say words that begin with the letter p. Solution. Move your mouth farther away from the microphone and turn your head away slightly. If you are using a wireless microphone, adjust it by moving it to another location near you. Visual Aid/Media Problems The more audiovisual equipment you use in your presentation, the more likely it is that something will go wrong. It is very important that you take the time to set up your equipment properly and make sure it is working. • Problem number 1. You accidentally drop your note cards and they get out of order. Solution. Make sure your note cards are numbered. In the event you drop them, you can quickly place them in their correct order. Try to do this without bringing attention to the notes. Also, do not have too many notes, so you don't have too many cards to shuffle. • Problem number 2. Your equipment stops working altogether. Solution. If you cannot quickly determine and correct the problem, continue your presentation without the visual aids. Don't make your audience wait while you fix the problem. If you absolutely need the visual aids, take a short break to correct the malfunction. 145 Expect the Unexpected • Problem number 3. Your slide carousel jams. Solution. Turn off the slide projector before you attempt to unjam the slide. Usually a slide gets stuck if it's not properly in line with the slide carousel. Use a pair of tweezers to remove the slide. • Problem number 4. The overhead projector bulb burns out. This is probably the most common overhead projector problem. Solution. Always have a spare bulb. Some of the better overhead projectors have a spare bulb built into the projector, and all you have to do is slide the bulb selection lever over for the new bulb. This works if (and only if) the spare bulb works and did not burn out when the last person used it. This has happened many times! Make sure you have a spare bulb, the correct spare bulb, and know how to change the bulb. Note: Keep in mind that the bulb currently in the projector may still be hot and you will burn yourself if you touch it. Unplug the projector and, using a towel or cloth, remove the old bulb and replace it with a new one. Since this can take a few minutes, I would suggest you call a break to give yourself time to do this without the entire room watching you fumble with the projector. Spend time during your initial setup learning how to change the bulb. You will be glad you did. Each projector is unique, and the procedure to change the bulb is different with each. If you do end up using the spare bulb, remember to have the hotel replace it so the next person does not get a surprise. 10 Days to More Confident Public Speaking 146 Room Lighting Many times it will be necessary to raise or lower the lighting in the room you are speaking in. Knowing where the lighting controls are and how to adjust the lighting is critical. • Problem number 1. The sconces (lighting fixtures on the wall) don't appear to have any switches to control them, and they cast a bright light. Solution. I have run across this problem a lot and usually end up having to loosen the light bulbs to turn them off. It may be that only one or two lights are causing the problem, but check out this detail during your setup. Platform Problems Sometimes it is necessary to speak from a raised platform or stage. Since most platforms are temporary and set up just for an event, it is important for your own safety to make sure the platform is properly supported. • Problem number 1. The platform is unstable. Solution. Walk the entire platform to check its sturdiness. Also, see how noisy the platform is when you walk across it. Check to make sure there are sturdy steps to walk up to the raised platform and that they are properly supported. Confidence Builder: Great Icebreakers Seldom is an icebreaker used when a keynote speech is given; however, most of you have probably attended a training session or seminar where you participated in an icebreaker game 147 Expect the Unexpected before the program started. Most of these icebreakers are intended to encourage participants to interact with one another. This is especially important if it's an all-day or multiday program. An icebreaker is used to stress a particular point or just to have fun. Here are some of my favorite icebreakers. Getting Acquainted Objective: To have first-time participants attending a training session get acquainted with one another and to help build a climate of friendliness among guests. Materials required: Blank stick-on tags. Approximate time required: Flexible, depending on the group size. Maximum time is fifteen minutes. Procedure: Give each person a blank name tag and ask each guest to write his or her first name or nickname on it. Have each guest list five words or brief phrases that describe something about him or her and can be used as conversation starters (residence, hobbies, children, and so on). Let's take a look at how my name tag would read. Name: Lenny 1. Connecticut resident 2. Professional speaker 3. Semiprofessional musician 4. Married 25 years 5. Two children After giving the group about five minutes to complete the task, have them separate into clusters of two and three. Every 10 Days to More Confident Public Speaking 148 few minutes tell the group to "change partners" in order to encourage everyone to meet as many people as possible. Discussion Questions Here's a list of questions to ask attendees once they have gotten to know one another. 1. Was this exercise helpful to you in getting to know some other people in the training session? 2. What kind of information had the greatest impact on you? 3. How do you now feel about your involvement in this group? Getting Acquainted Again It's okay to have your workshop participants meet one another more than once. Objective: To allow participants to become better acquainted through a structured exercise. Material required: Blank name tags. Approximate time required: Between fifteen and twenty minutes depending on the size of the group. Procedure: At the opening session of a group meeting, give each individual a blank name tag. Have each person complete the following items with five- or 10-word responses. 1. My name is ——. 2. I have a question about ——. 3. I can answer questions about ——. 149 Expect the Unexpected After a few minutes encourage attendees to seek out other attendees who can answer or be asked a question. Let the group mingle for ten to fifteen minutes. Camouflage for a Departure Here is an icebreaker to use at a large conference when you did not have the opportunity to do an audience questionnaire beforehand. It will allow attendees to bow out gracefully, if they realize they are in the wrong room. Objective: To ensure at a large conference that attendees select the right session and to allow an opportunity to quickly become acquainted with the attendees. Materials required: None. Approximate time required: Five minutes. Procedure: At large conferences the program description for individual sessions does not always accurately describe what the speaker or content will cover. Once the session starts, the attendees may discover the session is not what they originally thought but are reluctant to leave. This icebreaker takes care of that situation. At the start of the session, paraphrase the session description in the program book, include objectives, and briefly indicate precisely what the session covers. Say to your attendees, "There may be some people in the room who now realize this session may not cover what they thought it would. Since it may be awkward or uncomfortable to get up and leave, let's all stand now, meet a few new people, and those of you who want to excuse yourselves can do so easily." Then have the 10 Days to More Confident Public Speaking 150 group make three or four new acquaintances for two to three minutes. There are hundreds, if not thousands, of icebreakers and games you can include in your seminars. The best source for ideas is a series of books by Edward E. Scannell: • Games Trainers Play (McGraw-Hill, Inc., 1989) • Still More Games Trainers Play (McGraw-Hill, Inc., 1991) • More Games Trainers Play (McGraw-Hill, Inc., 1993) • Even Still More Games Trainers Play (McGraw-Hill, Inc., 1994) Tips from the Experts: How to Recognize and Take Advantage of a Spontaneous Moment Spontaneity is fundamental to the success of your presentation and plays an important role in your credibility. You lose a chance to connect with your audience by not taking advantage of a spontaneous opportunity. Tony Jeary, author of Inspire Any Audience, says a joke by an audience member, a piece of timely news, even a mistake you make, are all spontaneous moments you can use to win the respect of your audience and strengthen your credibility. The irony in spontaneity is that to be spontaneous, you have to be prepared. Mark Twain once said, "It takes about six weeks to prepare a good ad-lib comment." The truth is that you can plan spontaneity. Leave space for responding to the unexpected in your presentation. For example, don't be afraid to detour from your presentation to go in a promising direction opened up by a question from the audience. One example where I took advantage of a spontaneous 151 Expect the Unexpected moment was a speaking engagement in Poughkeepsie, New York, near the airport. I was talking about external noises and how they can be distracting. Just as I was discussing the various types of distractions, a jumbo jet flew over the hotel, making its usual loud noise. It got so loud, in fact, that I had to stop speaking. After the jet passed, I turned to the audience and said, "Do you know how much I paid that pilot to do that? I love it when people follow their cues on time." The audience was hysterical, and that moment really drove my point home. Outtakes: The Biggest Flub-ups and How the Speakers Covered Themselves In previous chapters I discussed the different methods you can use when delivering a speech and the importance of preparing properly. Despite completing both these objectives, you may one day find that your mind goes blank, you forget to bring a prop, or you encounter some other problem during your presentation. Here are examples and stories of real events gleaned from my membership in the National Speakers Association and how these professionals handled the situations. You Get Sidetracked in the Middle of the Talk There are three main reasons you may get sidetracked: • You don't have clear objectives. • You're not well prepared. • You get irrelevant questions. 10 Days to More Confident Public Speaking 152 To Prevent It from Happening Your objectives are crystal clear if you • firmly establish your exact mission. • develop a theme to support your mission. • simplify your presentation to three or four main points to support the mission. • make the "track" easy to follow, to help your audience follow your message. • rehearse, rehearse, rehearse. What to Do Here are responses from successful speakers when they are asked irrelevant questions from the audience. 1. Answer the question briefly with respect and compassion for your audience. Remember, your audience is your customer. Treat the attendees with care. 2. Quickly tie the seemingly irrelevant question back into your topic. When you find yourself getting sidetracked, check how much time you have left in your presentation. If there's a scheduled break, use the time to go over the presentation and decide what to cut or skip the break or create a really short break to compose yourself and ultimately save time. (Tip provided by Lilly Walters, author of Secrets of Successful Speakers, McGraw-Hill, Inc., 1993.) 153 Expect the Unexpected You Realize the Speaker Before You Has Already Told Your Story For example, I had the opportunity to attend a presentation Jeff Dewar was giving to Lockheed Corporation at its Los Angeles headquarters when he was presenting his famous statistics speech, "What Does 99.9 Percent Quality Mean to You?" He introduced several themed scenarios—how often we drink contaminated water, how efficiently the normal heart operates, and so on—then went on to say that if any of those scenarios were to function at a 99.9 percent level of quality, it would mean, for example, "you would be drinking unsafe water for one hour each month," "your heart would fail to beat thirty-two thousand times a year," "some twentytwo thousand checks would be deducted from the wrong bank account each day," and so forth. Usually this part of his talk is a big hit, but at Lockheed that day it fell flat. One of the attendees told Jeff afterward, "Sure seems like everybody is quoting from those 99.9 percent statistics." Swelling with pride, Jeff said, "Really? And where did you hear them before?" "Oh, the speaker this morning. He said he came up with them." Not fun. What to Do • Watch and feel the audience. If you see people looking slyly at one another, chances are something is wrong. • Casually stop, keep the mood you are trying to create in your tone of voice and mannerisms, and ask,

"Have you heard this before?" • Let the audience tell you. Turn it into a group sharing moment. Encourage your audience to tell you what an 10 Days to More Confident Public Speaking 154 earlier speaker said, then have them relate what they learned. • Do not say anything about the other presenter using your material, unless you deliver it as a compliment! You Trip on the Way to the Lectern Even though you think you're walking with care, your mind might be on your presentation, and you trip. To Prevent It from Happening Before you stand up to walk to the lectern: • Take a deep breath. • Stand up and walk. • Go slowly. Adrenaline is pumping through your system. Although you feel as if you're crawling to the lectern, your audience is seeing you scurry along at a good clip. What to Do First of all, know that the audience doesn't care that you tripped. However, they care if you get hurt, and they care if you make a scene about it. • Make a lighthearted remark about your stumble, and it will more than likely set the stage for a great presentation. An audience likes you better when you demonstrate that you have faults—especially if you are able to laugh at your own shortcomings or flub-ups. Here is a list of one-liners that can help you gloss over an embarrassing moment. • I also do magic tricks. • It took years of finishing school to learn to do that. 155 Expect the Unexpected • I'm the only speaker who can fall up a set of steps. • Is there a doctor in the house? • All that money I spent at Arthur Murray's was a waste. • I used to be too humble to stumble. • Give me an inch and I'll take a fall. (From One-Liners for Disasters, by Tom Antion, Anchor Publishing, 1993.) Sample Speech: The Ceremonial A ceremonial speech, also called a "testimonial speech," is given to honor a person or organization for something he or she has accomplished. For example, I gave the following speech, "Saying Good-Bye," during a snowstorm four years ago. I was honoring a fellow colleague who was retiring. Ladies and gentlemen, we are here today to honor a distinguished colleague of ours for his dedicated years of service to this company. Tom has been not only a colleague of mine, but also a friend. Tom and I go way back. In fact, we go so far back, they had to use old-fashioned dating techniques to verify Tom's age. (Ha, ha.) Tom has been with us for more than twenty years and has finally decided to retire. We are going to miss him dearly. Tom is only retiring from work, not from life. Tom is only beginning a new phase of life. I am so glad to see all of you who weathered the winter storm out there just to touch base with Tom before he moves on to better, bigger, and more exciting things. This speech was effective because I added humor and touched upon Tom's accomplishments and what he meant to the company.

One of the most important rules to follow on the day of your speech is to not radically change your normal schedule. Get plenty of rest the night before. When you wake up the next day, have a nutritious, well-balanced breakfast. A healthy breakfast gives you the physical and mental energy you need for the speaking engagement. More than likely you are nervous, and nervousness requires energy. Your body needs food to give you energy. The best food to eat is whole-grain cereals, fruit, toast, and bagels with a glass of juice. Do not eat a heavy meal like eggs and bacon.

CHAPTER TWELVE

Special Techniques for public speaking

I will provide you with an inside look at techniques I and other professional speakers use. By the end of this chapter you will know how to apply these ideas and tips to your presentation. Before you move forward with today's lessons, remember two things: First, the key is to use these techniques consistently. Second, public speaking is an acquired skill, and what you do before your presentation determines your success. In order to incorporate special techniques, you will need to review your body language, movement, gestures, tone of voice, and overall performance. Videotaping Yourself Here is a general plan of all the different aspects of speech giving you can critique with the four-step analysis. At certain times you may wish to use all of these video techniques—at others only one or two may be necessary. Once you are familiar with the process, you can use your own judgment depend- ing on the speech situation. Here is a list of elements to look for when reviewing your videotape: • Posture • Gestures • Body movement • Facial expressions • Eye contact • Voice Remember, the first step in eliminating any superfluous mannerisms or language is to get an accurate perception of your body language and voice. Sit with a notepad and write down everything you notice on the video about your body language and voice. • Review #1. Review the tape without looking for particular mannerisms. Just listen to the presentation as if you were hearing it for the first time and evaluate the overall impact you experience from watching the tape. During this initial review, pretend you are a member of the audience and evaluate your reaction to the presentation, trying to separate the fact that you are watching yourself. This will be difficult. Here are a few questions to think about and ask yourself during this review. —Did I like the presentation? —Was it informative or entertaining? —Would I recommend someone else watch this video? • Review #2. Turn off the sound and look only for visual distractions. Jot down notes on what you observe. Make two lists, one for the things you liked and another for the things you did not like. Don't worry if your list of 159 Special Techniques cons is longer; each time you give a presentation your performance will improve. Look specifically for the following: —What did you do with your hands? —What were your facial expressions? —What did you do with your body? —Did you move around? Did you stand still? —Were there any mannerisms you found distracting or annoying? —Did you seem appropriately animated? • Review #3. Darken the picture or turn your back to the TV so you cannot see yourself and listen only to your voice. Many people have never heard a taping of their own voice before except maybe on their answering machine. Become accustomed to listening to your voice. The first reaction I have had from most people when they hear themselves for the first time is, "That doesn't sound like me!" What happens is that when you hear your voice for the first time you are not hearing it from "inside" your head. While listening to your voice, focus on the following: —What do you like and not like about your voice? —How was the speed of your speaking? Was it too fast or too slow? —How was your tone of voice? —How was your pitch? Was it too high or too low? • Review #4. After you have completed your list of pros and cons, ask one or two family members to watch the tape with you. Get their initial impression. Have them take their own notes, and when the tape is finished compare your notes. Keep this list handy and tackle 10 Days to More Confident Public Speaking 160 each negative point one at a time. And remember the positive ones! Another important step is to gather all the notes and make another list. This is a list of those areas you believe need improvement. Make sure you are as specific as possible. Now take the items on the list and break them down into the following categories: • Voice and tone. This includes the tone of your voice, speed, pitch, and any verbal distractions such as uhms, uhs, ers, and ya knows. • Nonverbal actions. List them specifically by the parts of your body such as your hands, facial expressions, legs, arms, walking patterns, and so on. Don't be surprised if the list is long. That's okay. All novice speakers will have a long list when they first begin giving presentations. With practice, practice, and more practice, you eventually will see fewer areas in need of improvement. Look at the list and prioritize what areas you want to start working on immediately. Make a conscious note of these areas and observe and listen to how you speak during your everyday activities. The next time you are at a party, business meeting, or with a friend see if you notice any of these distracting mannerisms. Also, do you notice any of these distractions while talking on the telephone? Each time you speak, make an effort to eliminate or replace the distracting mannerism with a verbal or nonverbal technique. Practice every day. By making adjustments and changes in your everyday speaking style, you will find it easier to apply these strategies to your more formal speaking engagements such as a presentation at work, a toast at a wedding, or a speech to a large group. 161 Special Techniques Another helpful tip is to keep a journal after each presentation. Take a few moments to reflect on your speech. Make notes about your strengths and weaknesses and write a brief summary on your speech topic, the audience, and any other factors that will come in handy for future presentations. Visualization: Self-Talk One of the most effective techniques that I use myself and teach people in my seminars, workshops, and especially private coaching is visualization. Visualization is strongly tied to your own "self-talk." Self-talk is the conversation you have with yourself either in your head or out loud. If your self-talk is negative, destructive, or even invalid, your subconscious automatically accepts what you tell it. It doesn't say, Oh, that was inappropriate, you don't want that. Your mind records what you tell it, good or bad. It is imperative that you control your self-talk or it will control you. If you continue to have negative thoughts about yourself, you will sabotage any potential you have as a public speaker. Instead use positive selftalk: I can do this. When you start to visualize yourself as a success, you will succeed. The self-talk concept is the ability to relate or tie together your real performance as a speaker with your self-image as a speaker. This also relates directly back to your beliefs regarding speaking anxiety. Remember, it starts with what you call it and what you believe, right or wrong. Consider the pattern of a speaker who is not confident with his or her speaking ability. This speaker goes into the situation totally unprepared, hoping it will be different, expecting the worst. And when you expect the worst, that's exactly 10 Days to More Confident Public Speaking 162 what happens. Next thing you know, you hear yourself saying, See, I told you you would fail. Let's take a look at a different approach. Imagine you said to yourself, I am looking forward to this presentation because I know I put a lot of time and effort into it and I will succeed because I am prepared! You would be amazed how this thinking creates positive, confident results. Visualize yourself walking to the podium, stage, or lectern with confidence. The audience is listening to every word you are saying, glued to your next comment, and raising their hands because they want to hear more and ask interesting thought-provoking questions. If you start visualizing yourself as a success, over time you will see an improvement in your speaking style. Say It Out Loud The visualization process I just discussed is a powerful technique. However, rehearsing your presentation verbally, mentally, and physically is a key element to your success as a public speaker. If you want to "fine-tune" your body mentally and physically to a point where your mind and body are in sync, you need to act out your presentation. For example, I tell my clients to say their speech out loud while they're in the gym, taking a walk, preparing dinner, or driving in the car. This technique does three things: • It forces you to engage your mind and your mouth at the same time. Your mind is a funny thing. On occasion when you start to say something out loud, you find that your mouth takes over what you intended to say and what comes out surprises even you. 163 Special Techniques • When your speech or presentation is completely planned, find a room where you can say your speech out loud. For example, if you are speaking at school, try to find a classroom that is not being used. If you are speaking at a corporation, see if there is a conference room or lounge where you can have privacy. • Speak in the tone of voice, pitch, and volume you plan to use during the actual presentation. Lessons from Mom: Be Yourself I remember whenever I was assigned to tell a story in school, the night before, my mother would say to me, "Len, don't worry about what people think and how perfect you have to be, just be yourself, and tell your story." The best way to incorporate Mom's advice is to visualize and relive the event. As a speaker, when you focus on communicating with your audience and sharing ideas as opposed to focusing on your performance, the speaking process becomes easier. Don't start your presentation thinking, I wonder if they will like my presentation, or, I hope they don't think I am lousy, or, Oh no, they probably know more than I do and will be bored. All too often this negative self-talk is a major source of speech anxiety. You are your own worst enemy, and the sooner you think more positively and trust in your abilities because you did prepare, the sooner you'll realize the powerful role your thought process plays in your success as a speaker. When you tell any story, the best technique is to relate something personal for your audience. In addition, you need to act out your story for your audience. This is where facial expressions and 10 Days to More Confident Public Speaking 164 gestures come in handy. In this situation it's perfectly normal to exaggerate your gestures to drive your point home. Type of

Speech: Demonstrative A demonstration speech is similar to an informative speech, except you tell the audience how to do something. For a sample demonstration speech, I have decided to demonstrate how to organize your thoughts and ideas for your speeches. You will find this demonstration an integral part of organizing your presentation. This is an excerpt from a speech called "Mind Mapping" that I have taught to numerous clients. I have been using this technique for almost thirty years not only to deliver speeches, but to write articles and books. Take a single sheet of paper and draw a circle in the center of the paper. This is reserved for your speech title. Let's assume your speech has four main points. Draw four lines branching off from the circle in the center of the page. Each branch represents a main idea of your speech. Now draw two lines off each main idea branch. These lines are reserved for your key points. Label each one of your main idea lines with what you will discuss first, second, and so on. From each main idea, label the key point lines as "a" and "b" to indicate which point comes first. Once you have filled in all the lines, your speech is mapped out. The goal of this method is to get your ideas down on paper in an organized manner to help you deliver your speech. The After-Dinner Speech This is an example of another type of speech you may be asked to give someday. There are several kinds of after-dinner speeches. The specific topic of an after-dinner speech varies 165 Special Techniques according to the event but usually focuses on saying a few words of wisdom and encouragement, often to motivate people and leave them with a pleasant impression of the event. Here is an example of an after-dinner speech I gave to a large international sales force at the end of a four-day weekend of training. The company that hired me wanted me to motivate and inspire the attendees to use the presentation skills and training they had acquired over the weekend and apply them in their work environment. This is an abridged version of the speech, "The Motivation to I.N.S.P.I.R.E." When you are asked to think about what the word "inspire" means to you, you may not come up with the same meaning as the person sitting next to you. If I were to ask each of you in this room to define the word "inspire," we would get several variations as to the meaning. Here is my definition of inspire: "to have the ability to change attitudes." Your attitude will not change until someone motivates or inspires you to think differently, and that is what I am here to talk about tonight. I have devised an acronym for the word inspire. Using this acronym, I will tell you how you can apply the techniques you learned this weekend to your next presentation. • I stands for the word influence. As world-class salespeople and now world-class presenters, you have the opportunity to influence many people. Think about what your next goal is as a speaker. Is it to influence a buyer? Is it to influence a partner, or is it to influence or impress your boss? Whatever your goal is, rest assured, you will make an impression and you will influence people to think, but will you influence them to think correctly? • N stands for the word need. To be successful in all your speeches, you must fully understand and address your audience's needs. For example, does my audience need to know every statistic on the health care reform? Will my 10 Days to More Confident Public Speaking 166 audience need another visual aid to get my point? Am I belaboring one point for too long? • S stands for the word success. Stanford University conducted a study several years ago with successful salespeople, and here is what they found: • Preparation accounts for 75 percent of your presentation. • Breathing accounts for 15 percent of your presentation. • Mental focus accounts for 10 percent of your presentation. What does this mean? The study proves that 75 percent of your success as a speaker depends heavily on your preparation. In order to achieve success, you need to properly prepare and implement your ideas. • P stands for the word passion. You must have passion for your subject or you won't inspire anyone. At the same time, just being passionate about your topic will not guarantee success. P can also stand for preparation. Proper preparation, coupled with using a personal story, is an effective tool for inspiring your audience. • I stands for the word improve. You will not improve unless you practice, practice, practice. Practice what you learned over the last four days of this conference. Remember, practice is the key to improving. • R stands for the word rewards. You will find that when you do practice and rehearse the skills you have learned over the last several days, you are rewarded with a better presentation. In turn you will be a more effective salesperson. 167 Special Techniques • E stands for the word enthusiasm. I hope that this weekend has been an opportunity for you to learn, grow, and get enthused about giving presentations. Take your enthusiasm and channel that energy back into your presentations and you will inspire and motivate yourself and the audience you are addressing.

CHAPTER THIRTEEN

Behind the Scenes of public speaking

Your speech, props, and visual aids are ready. Now comes the final part of planning a speech or presentation— mental preparation. In order to deliver the best speech or presentation, you have to "psych" yourself up for the big moment. In this chapter I show you how to achieve this goal. Throughout the chapter I've sprinkled tips and strategies to show you how to become your own best coach, the importance of making a checklist, and a refresher lesson on the dos and don'ts of public speaking. In addition, you will learn how to deliver a persuasive speech—and for an added bonus, I teach you how to deliver bad news or negative results in a speech. Becoming Your Own Best Coach Although you've gotten feedback from family and friends on your speeches, ultimately you are responsible for coaching yourself through the speech process. Since your mind is a powerful machine, your body reacts to what your mind sug- gests. You are your own best coach. Your thoughts, either positive or negative, determine the success of your presentation. Therefore you need to continually strive for greatness in your speeches or presentations. If you have children or ever played a sport yourself, you know how exhilarating it is when a coach praises the team for a job well done. In public speaking you are not only the coach, but the team. It all rests on your shoulders. As your own coach, tell yourself every day that you are a winner in public speaking. Every day practice your techniques and strategies so you're ready for your next big speech. The Importance of Checklists Go the extra mile to make sure your speech or presentation is a grand slam. I make checklists for every presentation, seminar, or workshop I give. Since any one of a host of problems can sabotage your presentation, it is imperative that you not let the little things fall by the wayside. In my career as a public speaker, I have spoken at many conventions and conferences and witnessed presenters panic because they forgot their visual aids, can't find their handouts, or didn't get the name of the individual coordinating the meeting or the new location of the hotel or meeting center when it was changed at the last minute. These are mistakes that can frazzle your nerves. To prevent this from happening to you, here are examples of checklists I use. The Prespeech Checklist Use this checklist when you are planning to give a speech to an association or organization. "The sooner the better" is the motto you should follow when you are putting together 10 Days to More Confident Public Speaking 170 your prespeech checklist. As the date of your presentation draws closer, make sure to confirm the following points. • The actual date and time of the speech. Make sure the date and time of your speech is the same as when you sent the information to the meeting planner along with your precustom survey. Over the years I have experienced several occasions when the date and time have changed, especially when I wasn't the only speaker on the program. However, even if you are the only speaker on the program, contact the hotel or convention center at least one week prior to your presentation to make sure the date and time are accurate. Let me share a story of when a presenter didn't confirm the date and time. My colleague was scheduled to speak to a large crowd at an association meeting in June. He did not call or contact the organizer after the date was scheduled. The day before the scheduled presentation, he flew into the city where he was speaking. When he arrived at the hotel he asked if anyone else from the association had registered yet. When the hotel checked the reservations list, they told him they had no record of that association being scheduled to speak at the hotel. Naturally he was confused, and after several phone calls to members of the association he quickly learned that he had made a huge mistake. Yes, he was at the hotel on the correct date, but he had arrived a year early! Keep in mind that many associations schedule their meetings two or three years in advance, and it is not unusual for them to book speakers for the events at that same time. When he was contacted in March, my colleague had written down the date of the speech for 171 Behind the Scenes the upcoming June. Since he thought the presentation was only a few months away and he was never contacted again by the association, he assumed everything was all set. Boy, did he get a very expensive surprise! This story illustrates the necessity of confirming all dates, times, and locations. Once again, never assume anything when you are planning a speech or presentation. • Prepare enough copies of your handouts. Confirm the number of people attending your session. Either bring extra copies with you or make arrangements with the hotel or convention center to have the copies ready when you arrive. If you choose the latter route, send copies of your materials to the appropriate person at least a week prior to the event. Include a cover letter asking the hotel to hold the materials for you for the particular date. Call to follow up that the package arrived, and get the name of a contact person. Always put yourself in the audience's mind. I have attended seminars where there were not enough handouts. I felt cheated, and it did not leave a good first impression with me. When I'm the speaker, I call the day before to confirm the number of attendees and add a few extra copies just in case additional people decide to show up. Associations such as the New England Speakers Association conduct monthly meetings and always have walk-in registrations. Walk-ins can account for 30 percent of your attendance. I always take that factor into account and bring 30–50 percent more copies. Also, there will be times when your session runs concurrently with other sessions and participants may want a handout even though they cannot attend your 10 Days to More Confident Public Speaking 172 presentation. To accommodate them, leave extra copies at the back of the room. • Make a packing list. Make a list of everything you need to bring with you for the presentation. I advise doing this at least three days before the speaking engagement. Check each item off the list as you pack it. In doing this, you know everything is packed and ready to go and you won't panic on the day of the presentation. Bring a copy of the checklist with you. When you unpack you can check that everything made it into the box. If you are driving yourself to the presentation, load the materials into your car the day before. If you are flying to the location, have the seminar materials shipped to the location at least one week ahead of time, so in the event the boxes are misplaced or lost, there is time to track the shipment. Always send a tracking slip with the shipment and keep a copy for your records. Very important! If you are sending materials to a hotel, call the hotel and ask where shipments are stored and with whom you should speak to confirm their arrival. • Call one more time. On the day or evening before your presentation, call your contact person, meeting planner, or hotel staff member to confirm that there have been no changes, such as room location or starting time of your speech. It is not unusual for times and locations to change at the last minute. For example, I was hired as a speaker for an association meeting where the number of people who registered was higher than originally expected and the location was changed to accommodate a larger group. When you arrive at the hotel, doublecheck one more time. Also, if the number of attendees has greatly increased beyond the 30–50 percent you anticipate, have additional copies of your materials 173 Behind the Scenes made. If the hotel or convention center can't do it for you, ask if there is a local photocopy center nearby so you can arrange to have more copies made in plenty of time. Speech Day Checklist There are several tasks you can complete to ensure that you are properly prepared on the day of your speech. • Arrive early. Arrive early so you have time to unwind, find the room location, and check its setup. Although you provided a room layout in the earlier stages of your speech planning, it doesn't hurt to check, double-check, or even triple-check. For many of my presentations, I arrive the evening before and take care of the room setup that night. If possible, arrange to meet with someone from the organization staff and have dinner together. This gives you the chance to get to know him or her and review any last minute requests you have. For example, I can remember a speaking engagement where I was the closing keynote speaker for a week of training conducted for an international sales force. Some of these presenters were, not to my surprise, still making last minute changes to their presentations. They were monopolizing a room of computers that had been set up especially for the training week. As I walked around the room and introduced myself to some of the presenters, it became clear to me that they were in a panic. What happened was that a computer virus had infected the networked computers and many of the speakers had lost their presentation slides and were scrambling to duplicate them. During 10 Days to More Confident Public Speaking 174 my conversations with the speakers, I also learned that about 25 percent were named Mike. Arriving the night before paid off. I incorporated these two facts (computer virus and the name Mike) into my keynote speech the next day. I was a hit. Arriving early allowed me to further customize my presentation at the last minute. • Contact your liaison for the event. When you arrive, contact the person who hired you. Ask if he or she would like to meet you in the room where you are speaking to check over the details and any last-minute changes. • Unpack. As you unpack and set up your materials for your session, make sure you place your materials where they are accessible to you. Use your packing list to check off each item as you take care of it. Place handouts at the back of the room or wherever you deem logical. • Arrange for a pitcher of warm water. Arrange to have a pitcher and glass of warm water nearby. Drinking warm water not only helps wet your mouth, but also relaxes your vocal cords and muscles. Contrary to popular belief, drinking ice water only tightens up your voice muscles. Inquire with the hotel staff or meeting planner if you need an extra table for the pitcher and glass, especially if you are speaking from a lectern. • Check out your equipment. The last thing you do is check out your equipment. Make sure you have spare bulbs for the overhead projector if you are using one. Test out your writing implements to make sure they still work. Make sure your equipment does not obstruct the audience's view from any part of the room and that they can see you and your visual aids from where they are sitting. 175 Behind the Scenes Hopefully you can now relax before your speech or presentation; knowing that everything is in place, you can psych yourself up for the actual event. It is very hard to get pumped up if you are worrying about last minute details. Meet and Greet Again, arrive early to meet and greet as many participants as possible before your presentation. If there is a cocktail hour or a meet-and-greet session, make an effort to introduce yourself to as many people as you can before the program.

There are several tasks you can complete to ensure that you are properly prepared on the day of your speech. • Arrive early. Arrive early so you have time to unwind, find the room location, and check its setup. Although you provided a room layout in the earlier stages of your speech planning, it doesn't hurt to check, double-check, or even triple-check. For many of my presentations, I arrive the evening before and take care of the room setup that night. If possible, arrange to meet with someone from the organization staff and have dinner together. This gives you the chance to get to know him or her and review any last minute requests you have. For example, I can remember a speaking engagement where I was the closing keynote speaker for a week of training conducted for an international sales force. Some of these presenters were, not to my surprise, still making last minute changes to their presentations. They were monopolizing a room of computers that had been set up especially for the training week. As I walked around the room and introduced myself to some of the presenters, it became clear to me that they were in a panic. What happened was that a computer virus had infected the networked computers and many of the speakers had lost their presentation slides and were scrambling to duplicate them. During 10 Days to More Confident Public Speaking 174 my conversations with the speakers, I also learned that about 25 percent were named Mike. Arriving the night before paid off. I incorporated these two facts (computer virus and the name Mike) into my keynote speech the next day. I was a hit. Arriving early allowed me to further customize my presentation at the last minute. • Contact your liaison for the event. When you arrive, contact the person who hired you. Ask if he or she would like to meet you in the room where you are speaking to check over the details and any last-minute changes. • Unpack. As you unpack and set up your materials for your session, make sure you place your materials where they are accessible to you. Use your packing list to check off each item as you take care of it. Place handouts at the back of the room or wherever you deem logical. • Arrange for a pitcher of warm water. Arrange to have a pitcher and glass of warm water nearby. Drinking warm water not only helps wet your mouth, but also relaxes your vocal cords and muscles. Contrary to popular belief, drinking ice water only tightens up your voice muscles. Inquire with the hotel staff or meeting planner if you need an extra table for the pitcher and glass, especially if you are speaking from a lectern. • Check out your equipment. The last thing you do is check out your equipment. Make sure you have spare bulbs for the overhead projector if you are using one. Test out your writing implements to make sure they still work. Make sure your equipment does not obstruct the audience's view from any part of the room and that they can see you and your visual aids from where they are sitting. 175 Behind the Scenes Hopefully you can now relax before your speech or presentation; knowing that everything is in place, you can psych yourself up for the actual event. It is very hard to get pumped up if you are worrying about last minute details. Meet and Greet Again, arrive early to meet and greet as many participants as possible before your presentation. If there is a cocktail hour or a meet-and-greet session, make an effort to introduce yourself to as many people as you can before the program. Get to know as many of their names as possible and even go so far as to ask them what they are expecting during your presentation. These techniques allow you to listen to your audience's expectations and may remind you of personal stories you can incorporate into your presentation that relate to issues they bring up. Do not limit yourself to meeting and speaking only with the leaders of the organization, association, or company; get to know participants and their guests as well. Do not consume alcohol during the social hour. I avoid alcoholic beverages before I speak since it can affect my presentation. Hold your beverage in your left hand so your right hand is free to shake hands with people as you greet them. Top Ten List: The Ultimate Dos and Don'ts List Let's take a moment to review what you should and shouldn't do during your presentation. 10 Days to More Confident Public Speaking 176 1. Don't underestimate the time it takes to prepare a presentation. 2. Don't wait until the night before to put your presentation together. 3. Do prepare and rehearse your presentation. 4. Don't stay up all night worrying about your presentation. 5. Do double-check spelling on your visual aids. 6. Do drink lots of water to protect your speaking voice. 7. Do arrive early to properly set up for your presentation. 8. Do meet and greet as many people as you can before you speak. 9. Don't drink alcohol. This may affect your presentation. 10. Don't ever apologize for being nervous.

In a persuasive speech you are persuading the audience to make a change, such as how they think about conflict, or getting the audience to do something they do not do now. Here is an example of a persuasive speech—"Why Join Toastmasters International"—that I give during workshops and seminars. Why Join Toastmasters International Whatever your personal and professional goals are in life, your success depends on your ability to communicate effectively. If you learn to express yourself and your ideas in a clear and concise manner so you are heard, understood, and respected, then you possess the qualities of a leader. 177 Behind the Scenes Where can you go to obtain the necessary support and training to further develop your speaking skills? Wouldn't it be great to belong to an organization that helps you improve your speaking skills? Wouldn't you love to have someone provide you with positive and constructive feedback? You bet! For the last several years, I have been a member of Toastmasters International, an organization formed in 1924 specifically for this purpose. In fact, the organization has more than 170,000 members from a variety of occupations and backgrounds. This organization is not just for professional speakers, it is for everyone! Toastmasters International was founded by Dr. Ralph C. Smedley, who conceived and developed the idea of helping others speak more effectively and with more confidence. More clubs were formed, and Toastmasters International was incorporated under California law in December 1932. I hold the highest rank in the organization, Distinguished Toastmasters Designation (DTM). This achievement took years of dedication, service, and hard work but was well worth the effort. This program benefits more than three million people worldwide, and you can be the next member. The benefits you gain as a member can change your life. As a Toastmaster, you learn how to overcome the initial nervousness you feel when called upon to give a speech or presentation. You learn how to logically organize and present your ideas with conviction. You also learn how to improve your ability to listen to other people's ideas and evaluate them with constructive criticism. The confidence you gain shows not only in your formal presentations, but also in your everyday speaking situations. Toastmasters is a nonprofit organization, and the yearly membership fee is less than $100. There is an initial $16 new membership fee, along with $18 dues every six months plus any local club dues to cover expenses. This total is less than many one-day seminars you may have attended. Being a member of Toastmasters also helps you learn how to become a team leader and conduct meetings more effectively. Many of you, I'm sure, possess some of these skills already. Toastmasters only enhances them.Here is how Toastmasters works. Toastmaster organizations are either open to the public, referred to as "open club," or associated with a specific organization or company and restrict their membership to only employees, "closed club." Toastmaster groups meet weekly, monthly, or bimonthly. At these meetings, a group of twenty or more people meet for an hour to two hours, depending on the club. Each meeting provides members an opportunity to practice their speaking skills, whether it is running the meeting or serving as one of the scheduled speakers on the program for that meeting. Furthermore, there are other speaking opportunities for everyone in attendance. At the same time, you have fun, and without realizing it, you are improving your speaking skills. Each member receives a variety of manuals and resources along with access to videotapes and audiotapes on public speaking and leadership skills. In addition, you have access to some of the best resources you can find—its members. Every member has the same goal—to become a more effective speaker—and Toastmasters provides you with a format that has a proven track record. I'm sure many of you are members of an association, school, or church committee where you are required to make presentations or speeches. Toastmasters helps you succeed in these roles as well. If you are anxious to improve quickly, you can. If you want to progress at a more leisurely pace, you can do that, too. Toastmasters is not a classroom; rather, it is a workshop for you to develop your communication and leadership skills among friends. Not convinced? Visit any Toastmasters meeting as a guest and see for yourself. You only need to find a club near you, find out when and where they meet, and show up. Becoming a member of Toastmasters is easy. There is probably a Toastmasters Club meeting in your town or a neighboring town. To locate a Toastmasters club near you and find more information, visit their Web site at www.toastmasters. org, or call them at 800-993-7732 to request information by mail. I can say truthfully, if it wasn't for Toastmasters, I would not be a professional speaker today. I also know that without the experiences I gained from Toastmasters, I would not have 179 Behind the Scenes developed and honed my speaking skills. So here is your call to action. This persuasive speech was a success because I told the audience about the numerous benefits of the program and asked thought-provoking questions, getting them to evaluate their own speaking skills. Types of Speeches: Reporting on Negative Results or Bad News One of the most difficult speeches to give is one in which you are required to deliver bad news or negative results. Often this type of speech is given by a person lower in an organization who needs to inform the higher-ups of a problem. The best approach when faced with this challenge is to prepare a presentation containing the pertinent details and facts. Above all, the best advice is to let the facts speak for themselves. In my former engineering career, I often had to make a presentation about a project that was not going as planned, and I had to consider whether obtaining more information or changing direction was the way to go. Let's review the general format to use in this instance, and then I will give an example using these guidelines. The objectives of most presentations that involve negative or bad news is to • inform the management of specific events, results, or issues. • make recommendations. • get support and direction from management. In some cases specific recommendations are unknown until you are advised by upper management. However, in my 10 Days to More Confident Public Speaking 180 experience, if you identify a problem and give recommendations as to what you would do, it is easier for management to endorse the solution or indicate that they want to study the results and make their own recommendations. In most cases they welcome the fact that you took the initiative to come up with solutions. Here's an example of a time when I had to inform management of an engineering analysis I just completed. Someone had indicated to management that a materials engineering review was not performed and they needed the review and approval of a design before installation. I was approached, and after reviewing the data test results for about two weeks, I realized that there were problems with the current design because improper materials were used. I was under the gun to complete this review and found myself pressured to approve the design. I knew that what I was going to tell management would not be considered good news, since it would mean a delay in the completion of the project. However, it was more important for management to know all the facts so they could make the final decision. I requested that I have an opportunity to make a presentation to management and explain my findings and results. Here's the structure I used for the meeting. • I presented an overview of the objectives of the engineering review and study, including the desired results of the review—approval of the material selection. • I described what I specifically reviewed and analyzed and against what criteria. I defined what was and wasn't acceptable regarding the results. • I pointed out where the test results were not what I would expect. I discussed why the test failures were significant and what the consequences meant in terms of the design. In this case, the materials needed to be 181 Behind the Scenes replaced with the appropriate ones, and I gave specific recommendations to correct the problem. • I outlined the various options I would pursue were I the decision maker and stated my recommendations as to the approach to take, along with the risks involved if other alternatives were considered. Since cost was a big factor, I included a detailed cost analysis for each option. • I indicated the preferred option and what was needed to implement it, along with a schedule. This option would delay the project by several weeks. I also described what I believed was the next best option, again with the cost schedule. Management will likely support you either way. In my case, I found some additional ways to expedite the schedule and replace the components. In the end, the project did not lose a significant amount of time. Later, upper management sent me a memo thanking me for being so thorough and honest and for allowing them to have a part in the decision. To sum up what you do in situations like the one I just shared: • Provide all the facts. • Do not lay blame on anyone. • Provide specific recommendations.

CHAPTER FOURTEEN

Public Speaking Tips You Can't Afford To Ignore

The speech starts with your bio before you walk on stage. That means that your introduction (which is often known as your "bio" in the trade) should be over-the-top powerful and impressive. Don't worry about being bombastic or selfcongratulatory: you can immediately disarm the audience with something sincere and selfeffacing as soon as you open your mouth. A disembodied announcer or the person who invited you will normally give your bio. It's fine — in fact, it's great — if they introduce you with gushing praise. It sounds a bit phony if you talk about yourself that way.You DON'T have to tell them what you're going to tell them. You've probably heard it before: "Tell 'em what you're going to tell 'em. Tell 'em. Tell 'em what you've told 'em." That's not necessarily bad advice. But it doesn't have to be that way. After all, every other speaker is doing it. If you're going to make your audience sit up and pay attention, wouldn't it be worth doing something that every other speaker isn't doing? Try a pattern-interrupt instead. Open with a surprise, a shock, or an interaction. Open with something that makes a connection, or something that entertains, or something that leaves you exposed. Be different. Be memorable. Cut, cut, cut! I often see (and you often see) extraneous detail added into stories and speeches that disrupt the flow. Cut to the meat. Cut to the chase. Include specifics at critical parts of the story. You don't need to pad out your speech to make an impact. Instead, you need to focus – with intention – on what's important. Your audience needs a lot less information to get to the "aha" moment than you might think.

An entire story is designed to serve the end. Whatever precedes the punch line must serve the pay-off. See point 3. Do I need to know what color socks you're wearing? Or how long it took you to get here today?Establish right away that you know what the world looks like for them—and what it could look like. Vividly paint the picture. All world-saving performances are transformational experiences for your audience. Start out by showing "here's what you've got today, and here's how it could be." This builds immediate rapport and hooks the audience's interest. You know them. You understand them. You've got their back ... and you've got a better way.

You must reward them for doing something or contributing in some way. Don't encourage interaction just to ignore it. Your audience isn't made up of dumb animals: they don't need treats. Instead, they're sentient and intelligent living beings who need simple acknowledgement. Imagine being asked to participate in something – whether it's holding a door open for a friend or running a project – and not even getting a nod of thanks in return. You start to feel bad right away. Use open hands with your palms up instead of your finger for pointing. Sometimes the finger looks like a gun. It's also rude in some cultures. Instead, extend your hands with your palms up as if offering up alms. It's more gracious, more inclusive and more giving. People say "yes" when we've affected them intellectually, emotionally or physically. Can you include those three elements in your presentation? Can you give them intellectual gristle to chew on? Can you make them gasp or cry or laugh with an emotional connection? Can you get them physically engaged (you can tell by the way they're sitting) with your ideas and message? If not, learn how and start today.

Outline your content and then unpack it. If you're teaching content (which is distinct from a "message") outline first, then go back and unpack it. This isn't the same as "tell 'em what you're going to tell 'em." It's a learning plan for what's coming next. It serves as both high-level overview before you get granular, and a teaser for the exciting content still to come. Use props. What can you show or demonstrate or depict with objects rather than words? Can you ethically assault your audience's visual senses as well as their auditory senses? Props aid recall: if you want to be remembered, you can be visually arresting (without dying your hair bright red) by using props to drive your point home. Most speakers don't do this. That's just one of the reasons why you should. Use contrast and extremes to create excitement and keep attention. Contrast can be emotional, physical and structural. This basic story-arc technique is integral to every great play, every great film, and every great piece of music.

Consider your performance like a roller-coaster ride. Can you take me to the edge of a cliff before artfully lowering me, with love and care, to a safe place? Can you make the highs higher and the lows lower? Keep moving forward. Never let the energy drop. You're on stage to take your audience to their final destination. Keep your foot on the gas pedal. You'll have uphill moments when your speed drops, but the power and intensity increase. You can be both calm and energetic. Practice

Audiences like to think that events on the stage are happening spontaneously. They like to be surprised. The great actor does this brilliantly. You, as a speaker, need to do this as well. The best way to be effortlessly spontaneous is to rehearse to the point of mastery. How often do you have to stop and think about "spontaneously" adjusting your shoelaces? Never. Because you know the role inside out. When you know your material you can deliver it like it's the first time, every time you perform it.

Stand and land. Let your punch lines, point lines, and purpose lines land. That means you don't move while you're delivering them. You remain physically rooted to the spot so that your body reinforces the gravity of your words.

You can move and talk at the same time. People do it all the time in real life. The idea that you can't walk and talk at the same time is ridiculous. But don't sway, and don't move when you're landing on your most important points (see "Stand and Land").

Don't say, "I'm glad to be here." Show them that you're glad to be there instead. Your audience should see it in your actions and hear it in your words. Besides, what's the alternative? That you're not glad to be there? Don't insult their intelligence.

Don't tell them you're going to tell a story. Just tell the story.

Every rule is made to be broken. But to break the rules of performance, you need to know what the rules are. You need to know why they exist and exactly why you're breaking them. When you break the rules with purpose, you can produce a better and more effective result. Bertolt Brecht was famous for regularly breaking the "rule" of the fourth wall and he got powerful results. Be very conscientious about connecting the dots or you'll lose your audience. If you're presenting a series of interconnected concepts or stories or characters, make it as simple as possible to understand. Remember: even though you know your story inside out, your audience is hearing it for the first time.

Give them time. If you like to encourage note-taking during your performance, make sure you give people enough to time write down what you want them to write down. Spell things out if necessary. You'll lose your audience very quickly if they've got their heads stuck in their notebooks or laptops. Never apologize for the amount of time you don't have. The minute you apologize for what they're not getting, your audience will start to feel that they're missing out on something. They should feel that the amount of time you have is the perfect amount of time. You can blow their mind in just a few minutes. Look at all those great TED talks for inspiration. Let them go early. Audiences love to be let out a few minutes early—even if they LOVE your performance. There are no prizes for endurance in performance. Let them leave a few minutes ahead of schedule. This is especially important if you've started late (through no fault of your own, of course).

Enlist the self-proclaimed experts in the room. There's always somebody who knows more than you – or thinks they do. Get them on your side. Talk them up. Kill them with lavish praise. It'll help knock the chips off their shoulders and get them supporting your message. Embellishment is positively OK. You can paint a more vivid picture with brighter colors. It's a performance, a show. Be honest, but remember you're not performing under oath, for goodness' sake. You can combine multiple stories into one story if it produces a better result. Go for what is most dramatic and effective to get your message across.

Remember they don't know what you know. It's the first time they've heard your info (see point 19). That means even though you're the expert, you're talking to interested students, not peers. Don't assume prior knowledge. It can only help your message if you're comprehensive. Don't use acronyms, or if you do, explain them the first time round. Show them what the world will look like if they DON'T change. Make it clear that if they don't follow your advice, or come with you on your journey, then their world will remain the same – if not get considerably worse – than it is today. Study stand-up comedy. Watch stand up comedians. Watch their set-up, delivery and pay-off. See how they own the stage. Stand up comedians can turn a water bottle into a tool for creating magic moments.

Be careful using idioms. Across cultures – even cultures that share a language – there are big idiomatic differences that can turn your message opaque for an audience who doesn't "get it." If you're an American talking to a British audience about bangs, bleachers, boondoggles or fanny-packs then you've likely lost them already. Don't make jokes about difficult topics. Even the most skilled stand up comedians have a tough time landing jokes about difficult topics that are awkward, sensitive, or otherwise confronting. If you want to make yourself the butt of your jokes, that kind of self-deprecating humor can work very well. Suicide is not funny. That doesn't mean you can't lighten up the mood when talking about difficult subjects but that's different than poking fun or making jokes.

If you tell them you care about something you also need to tell them why. It's not good enough to say, "I'm a strong proponent of women's rights." You've got to hook them in with your reasons. Your why is what makes your beliefs more powerful and your cause stronger. Boom, boom, BANG. Boom, boom, boom, BANG. The rule of three is one of the rules of performance you need to know how to use. It's powerful, it's potent, and it packs a punch (see what I did there?) Understand stage blocking. You need to remain physically open so everyone in the room can see you at all times. That means you don't hide or turn to face anybody other than your audience ... unless for dramatic effect.

Deliver big moments center stage (usually). Centering yourself physically on the stage is the same as bolding and centering a headline in a newspaper. It says: "this is important – pay attention." When you designate center stage as the pivotal point for your performance, you can more effectively use the rest of the stage to support your main message. There are always exceptions to this concept. That said, don't head straight for center stage. When coming on stage for the first time, avoid making a beeline directly to center of stage and then starting your speech. It looks stiff, clunky and amateurish. Lean how to rehearse. Rehearsal is key to performance. It's not just repetition, but training. If you have to stop when you're rehearsing, start back up at the exact same emotional, physical and energetic state. Otherwise, you'll lose the through-line and arc of the speech.

When you land a joke, bask in it. If public speaking is notoriously difficult, making people laugh when you're performing is devilishly tough. Make the most of your moments in the spotlight. Voice and speech training is not something you master in an hour. I studied daily for three years in a Master of Fine Arts acting program at NYU. True performers never stop learning. Voice and speech training is mandatory for all performers, not least for their physical health. Sure, we've all heard stories about accidental film stars who were spotted in line at Starbucks. But they'll always be the exception (which is why it makes for such a good story). Don't push. (Push is a theater term for over-acting.) When you push, you can't show emotion. When you push, the work feels false and selfobsessed. It's insincere.

Insincerity is the enemy of truth. Truth is integral to performance.

Just because you're feeling it, they might not be. Major emotion for you as the speaker doesn't always translate to major emotion for your audience. It's only in rehearsal and practice that we find out what works and what doesn't. You might be moved to tears while your audience is bored to tears. Endings: get everything in before audiences clap. Then, get off the stage quickly. Don't let them see you doing housekeeping. It breaks the theatrical experience. You're the performer. They're not interested in watching you collect questionnaires. You can also stay on stage at the end if you invite them to join you there. That way you're "hosting the party." You don't want them grabbing you in the restroom: nothing dissipates magic like a damp handshake in the gents.

Anyone can make a sexy sizzle reel. Meeting planners want to know you can "hold the stage" for an extended period of time. Make sure you can show them video of 5-15 minutes of continuous performance where you deliver a message and engage the audience. No speaker gets hired just because they have a good video editor. Get right to it. Most speakers waste time on too much exposition and preparation and the audience starts thinking, "Let's go already!" Instead, hit the accelerator hard and launch straight on as you mean to continue. Let them know what they're in for by what they experience from you in the first 30 seconds. Stop using the "story teller voice." It's false. You tell a story to 10,000 the same way you tell the story to your best friend. You don't use some dramatic made-up voice. It's another mark of an amateur. Study your favorite speakers. It's like there are just the two of you in the room.

You have no time for self-indulgence. You must be clinical and surgical with your material and your message. Don't use overly obfuscating verbiage when you can say things simply. We get attached to bits that really don't further the story or resonate with the audience, perhaps because they're funny or easy for us or have a special meaning to us. But it's not about us. It's never about us. It's about them.

You don't have to slow down. Most speaking teachers tell you to slow down. Sometimes that makes sense. But if we're worried about speed, we're focused on the wrong thing. Instead of slowing down, focus on pausing. Speakers that speak too slowly have a soporific effect. I speak quickly. And I pause at the right places. That creates rhythm. I slow down when it serves the speech to slow down. Remember how contrast creates compelling theatrical experiences? One note, even the most beautiful note, gets boring over time. Audiences can easily absorb the important points if you give them pause time

If you have to explain a joke... It's just not funny. No joke gets funnier with explanation. Choose a better joke or let it go altogether. Never turn your back to the audience unless it's intentional to make a point or convey an emotion. When you need to move upstage (that's toward the back of the stage, away from the audience) you walk backwards. Never yell at your audience. This shouldn't need saying, but we sometimes let our standards slip when we're not in "performance mode." You're ALWAYS performing when you're in front of a group of people. If you need to get everybody's attention after a coffee break, say, simply raise your hand and stand silently. People will follow. That's powerful.

If you think you're going to rise to the moment, you're wrong. Under pressure, you don't rise to the occasion; you fall back on your training. If you think you're going to come up with the right material during the speech without hours of preparation, think again. You must be prepared beyond preparation if you want to make life-saving, world-changing speeches.

CHAPTER FIFTEEN

WHAT FEAR DOES TO US DURING A SPEECH

Being nervous during a public speaking event affects the way we come across to an audience and the quality of our delivery. Nervous speakers tend to talk too quickly and generally ignore the audience, focusing instead on their presentation slides or the floor.They talk in a flat voice, with little excitement or vocal pitch variation, and they try to get through the experience without committing to the speech or presentation. TALK TOO QUICKLY AND IN A MONOTONE Rushing through a talk requires that you talk fast and talking fast interferes with your breathing. Instead of breathing comfortably, you breathe in a short, shallow manner, or you might even hold your breath. This gives you the sensation of running out of air and being unable to breathe, a common fear in this situation, and one that greatly increases fear of public speaking.Talking quickly reduces the chance the audience can enjoy your speech. It creates a barrier between you and them, as they might struggle to understand what you are saying. Here are some common issues with talking too quickly: • You won't be breathing deeply enough to fill your lungs with air • You'll sound monotone due to lack of vocal range and air in your lungs • You'll sound nervous to the audience • The audience will struggle to understand what you are sayingOver 75% of people experience some level of anxiety when speaking in public Remember, the human voice is in theory capable of paying 24 notes on the musical scale. Most people only use 3 in their everyday speech so if you can incorporate more then you're already well on your way to becoming an interesting and engaging public speaker.

IGNORE THE AUDIENCE AND AVOID EYE CONTACT Fearful speakers often try to ignore the audience, hoping this will decrease their speech anxiety. For instance, lots of speakers avoid eye contact with the audience.

This prevents you from noticing any audience reactions. You won't notice when people seem more interested or have questions. When you have no audience contact, you focus on your own thoughts. And if you're a nervous speaker, your thoughts are virtually guaranteed to be far more negative, and unrealistic, than anything your audience might think or say. FIGHT TO HIDE YOUR FEAR Finally, efforts to hide your fear create the additional fear of being "found out" as a nervous person. This only adds to the public speaking anxiety you already experience. It has another negative side effect. After you've given a speech, even if it has gone well, you may not feel like it was a success because you think: "If the audience knew how afraid I was, they'd think less of the presentation."

Despite many people fearing speaking in public, communication skills are essential in the workplace: 83% of human resource directors saying employees who couldn't develop social skills would not become high performers. So, if you manage to overcome your fear of public speaking, this is a brilliant skill for your resume and you'll be able to accelerate more quickly in your career, as well as be more confident in your personal life. The core of being a great public speaker lies predominantly in one thing: confidence.

WHY DO WE HAVE THIS FEAR?

Let's discuss how this fear comes about and why so many of us fear speaking in public. Understanding the root cause will hopefully help you deal with it better.

In the book, "Confessions of a Public Speaker" by Scott Berkun, he suggests that our brains identify the following four conditions as extremely bad for survival: • Standing alone • In an open territory with no place to hide • Being without a weapon • In front of a large crowd who are staring at you These conditions made sense during the early years of humans. Being alone, or without a weapon for example, could have been very dangerous with wild animals and other fierce tribes nearby. There conditions happen to all be experienced during public speaking. You're often alone on a stage, open to the audience who are looking at you, without a weapon and with nowhere to hide (assuming you don't hide behind your laptop). So, what exactly can you do to gradually overcome the fear of public speaking? Here are key tips that you can apply before, during and after the speech.

8 TIPS TO OVERCOME YOUR FEAR OF PUBLIC SPEAKING

1. PRACTICE ALOUD This is the most important point – you need to practice, over and over again. You can practice in front of friends or

family for feedback, join your local Toastmasters club or use a virtual reality (VR) app. VR apps are highly effective at tricking the brain into thinking the audience in the app is real. Methods of practicing aloud: • Join a local Toastmasters club • Give a speech in virtual reality • Present to a friend or colleague • Practice in web-based simulations • Practice with a mirror (ideally full length) • Practice on a video conferencing simulation This is a great way of bridging the gap between practicing in front of a mirror to practicing in front of a group of people (something that you might avoid altogether depending on your fear of public speaking). 2. REMEMBER WHY YOU'RE THERE Usually, you are on stage because people value your expertise and knowledge - or at the very least, whoever has put you there has confidence in your capability. You might be speaking about a recent publication, or a branch of research you successfully tested. Use this thought to try and relax - people aren't there to give you a hard time. In fact, most people are probably just grateful it's you speaking on stage and not them! To ensure you connect with your audience, you need to plan your speech accordingly. For example, don't use jargon or acronyms if your audience is from a different industry to yours. Keep your language and your slides as simple as possible.

3. HAVE A SCRIPT, BUT DON'T MEMORIZE IT What are people most afraid of? Forgetting what to say in front of hundreds of people. Even the most notable public speakers in history have used scripts, forgotten what they were going to say, and then panicked. The fear of public speaking can consume all we think about. This might seem really daunting at first and will increase your anxiety levels just thinking about not having the safety of a script. However, remember that when you have a script you tend to either read from it (and therefore lose your connection with the audience) or you memorize it word for word. The problem with the second method is that if you lose your place, you'll panic, stumble, and not know what to say next. A better approach is to make your script into a series of bullet points or, better yet, a list of themes or connecting sentences on a cue card. This will make the speech sounds more authentic and less rehearsed, and you'll be more likely to show your passion for your topic when speaking from your heart rather than your head. Method for going from a topic to a speech Start with a rough outline of the topic you want to talk about. Type up this outline in a conversational style and read it aloud several times to yourself. When certain parts of the speech don't sound right, correct the outline accordingly. As you keep rehearsing, try to use your written outline

less and less. Highlight certain keywords and phrases you need to mention and add those to cue cards or something similar. Now start practicing with just the cue cards as you would when speaking at an actual event. On the day of the event, keep the cue cards as backup, maybe next to your laptop, and you'll be able to speak much more naturally than if you had rehearsed from a script. 4. DON'T RELY ON TECHNOLOGY If there was something more nerve wracking than forgetting the lines of your speech, it would be for a live demo to fail. It is a horrible, gut-wrenching feeling. One way to have more confidence and reduce your fear of public speaking on the day is to make sure you have a backup such as a video showing of your presentation or a second method of presentation. For example, if you're using PowerPoint software and the computer or projector isn't working, it can be handy to have printed out the presentation for the audience (and yourself if you need it). Similarly, you should import your presentation offline so that if the internet doesn't work, you can still present without becoming flustered. What can go wrong with technology during a speech: • Embedded videos might not play or have no sound • The presentation pointer / clicker may stop responding • Projector doesn't link to your laptop • Any live demo may fail (an example being the face recognition for the iPhone X demo)

5. KNOW YOUR AUDIENCE The type of audience you'll be facing affects your choice of language, humor, opening sentences, length and many more. There are several ways to understand the audience you're speaking to: • Research the event using their social media and blog posts • Learn about the other speakers (if it's a conference) and the types of presentations they are giving • Greet audience members when they enter the room and ask them a few questions about their background, expertise, what they expect etc. • Find out the size of the audience (this may determine the structure of your speech, including where to do the question-and-answer session, whether to include humor etc.) Once you understand your audience, you'll feel more confident about the questions and answers session at the end and that you are delivering a speech the audience actually want to hear. • How to analyze your audience before a presentation • Guide to choosing a successful speech topic 6. PAUSE AND TAKE DEEP BREATHS This simple advice cannot be emphasized enough. When you're nervous, you breathe rapidly and shallowly. This is telling the audience that you're not confident. Slow and measured breathing is a sign that you're in control. Before you go to the front of the room, concentrate on taking a few slow breaths. Repeat

this several times. When you start to speak, remember to pause, and breathe after you make a point. It's important to remember that there is nothing wrong with a bit of silence during a speech. It can actually be a good thing and bring emphasis to what you've just said. Be aware that on stage, pausing for just a few seconds can seem like a very long time – resist the urge to break the silence for at least 3 seconds. • 10 effective ways to use pauses in your speech 7. CREATE BACKUP SLIDES FOR AUDIENCE QUESTIONS One reason people often experience anxiety before a presentation is the fear that they'll be asked questions that might be difficult to answer. Don't get caught off guard. Think carefully about potential questions that might arise and rehearse the answers. Go one step further by creating slides for some potential questions about complex issues. In your extra slides, you can include important information, numbers, stats or even an interesting graph or pie chart that would be helpful to the audience. If such a question arises, it's okay to say, "I thought I might be asked this question and I've got a slide which explains it well..."

90% of the anxiety we feel before making a presentation comes from lack of preparation

8. FOCUS ON THE BEGINNING AND ENDING Your opening sets the tone for your speech and your closing is what you will leave your audience with. You'll have a few seconds when you start to capture the attention of the audience and prevent them returning to their mobiles. Therefore, you need to make it good. Try starting with an attention-grabbing statement, statistic, or interesting quote. • How to start a presentation effectively The ending brings the presentation to full circle and is when your audience's attention peaks again. This may be one of the few sections they remember so it's important you get it right. • Different ways to end a presentation or speech Rather than leaving the opening and ending to chance, write and practice them repeatedly. What you can do is memorize certain sentences or phrases you think are key to your speech and note down bullet points of other information you want to include in these sections.

BEFORE THE PUBLIC SPEAKING EVENT Use these tips to help deal with your fear before an event: • Greet audience members as they enter the room you'll be presenting in. Knowing a few of them before you start will ensure you have a few friendly faces you can look at during the presentation • Complete the breathing exercises detailed below this section to slow down your heartrate • Check that your slides and laptop are working with the projector • Drink some water to prevent a dry mouth • Perform some vocal exercises to warm up your voice before a speech AFTER THE PUBLIC SPEAKING EVENT It's a good idea to reflect on your speech afterwards. Dale Carnegie once said about public speaking, "There are always three speeches, for every one you actually gave. The one you practiced, the one you gave, and the one you wish you gave." For that speech you wish you gave, this is why you need to invest some time to reflect in your performance. Be honest with yourself on three points – what was good about your speech, what didn't work about your speech and what could have been improved? If you have trusted friends who were part of your audience, run through these questions with them to obtain a better and more diverse perspective. Better still, record all your speeches and review them personally. Yes, it can be painful, and you will probably cringe while watching yourself on video or listening back to an audio recording. But this process is absolutely necessary for you to become a better speaker and one who is committed to overcoming their fears of speaking.Fear of public speaking inhibits promotion to management by 15%

THE CURE FOR INSECURITY IS PREPARATION AND EXPERIENCE The key to overcoming your fear of public speaking is preparation and experience. Solid preparation will leave you feeling more confident in your ability as an excellent public speaker, able to deliver a clear, engaging speech. Experience will help you become more comfortable with the whole experience and stop you dreading that presentation. You'll need to get out there and speak in public a few times, so join a local Toastmasters, volunteer to speak at a conference, practice in VirtualSpeech simulations or try any other method of overcoming your fear of public speaking.

CHAPTER SIXTEEN

Four Types of Speech Delivery

There are four types of speeches that most speakers utilize in delivering a speech. 1. Extemporaneous speeches are speeches that are carefully prepared and practiced by the speaker before the actual speaking time. A speaker will utilize notes or an outline as a guide while they are delivering the speech. The notes or outline will usually include any quotes and sources the speaker wants to cite in the presentation, as well as the order the information in the speech should be delivered in. The speech is delivered as if the speaker is having a conversation with the audience. Since the speaker is not reading the entire speech, the extemporaneous speaker uses the notes as a guide only – a sort of memory trigger – and the speaker will also be able to respond to the audience since her head isn't trapped by reading every word on a paper. This is the type of public speaking you should strive to use in Fundamentals of Oral Communication for your informative and persuasive speeches as this is most practical type of public speaking – the type you are most likely use in a real life situation when you might be asked to give a formal presentation. It used to be a pretty standard technique of putting your notes or outline on notecards – those 3" by 5" recipe cards. The idea was that the palm of your hand can hold 3 by 5 inch cards and they won't be distracting to an audience – in fact, if you hold them just right, an audience almost can't see what is in your hand. Since the cards are relatively small, you would need several note cards for a ten minute speech (probably around five at least). I tend to have a Murphy's Law sort of experience is I speak off of note cards – they can be in the right order when I'm at my seat but by the time I get to the podium to speak one will be in the wrong order or worse yet, it will be gone entirely – zapped into the ozone! With the advent of computers, I find it is easier for me to use a single sheet of computer paper with an outline or list of notes to speak off of. I recommend that students use what they are comfortable with to speak off of. So, for this course, use either note cards or a single sheet of computer paper for your presentations.

2. Impromptu speeches are speeches that are delivered without notes or a plan, and without any formal preparation – they are very spontaneously delivered. This is one of the most nerve wracking situations for most students to find themselves in because there isn't a plan or agenda to follow – they just have to get up and speak without any "thinking" time. They are afraid of not knowing what to say when they get up in front of the audience so they might make a fool of themselves. If this type of speaking situation makes you nervous, you are not alone! The reality is that this is the type of public speaking you are the MOST prepared for. Your daily life is filled with impromptu experiences and conversations. Every phone conversation, exchange between you and a loved one, and discussion amongst friends is impromptu by its very nature – even if we "practice" our conversations, they are still impromptu in their delivery. So, while most students are nervous about impromptu speeches, they are the type they are the most prepared for from their daily experience. 3. Manuscript speeches are speeches that are delivered with a script of the exact words to be used. If they have to give a speech, most students prefer to have every single word in front of them so they can basically "read" the speech to the audience. While this is very reassuring for a speaker and they feel like they won't "forget" anything if they have every word in front of them, manuscript speaking is one of the worst traps to fall into for a speaker. The speaker who utilizes a complete manuscript will often spend more time looking at the script than at the audience. By doing this, the speaker is unable to react to the audience or respond to the audience members questions. Therefore, the manuscript becomes a trap for the speaker. 4. Memorized speeches are speeches that are committed to memory. The speaker completely memorizes the text of a speech and then delivers the speech from memory without reliance on notes or an outline. This is a very fearful speaking situation for most people because they fear they will forget what they had planned on saying when they get in front of the group – and, they might make a fool of themselves in front of the audience if they forget what to say. This type of speaking is not very common to daily living unless you are in a profession like acting. Most of us memorize very little in our daily lives – we don't even have to remember telephone numbers since we have cellular phones! I don't require

memorized speeches for Fundamentals of Oral Communication because I think they lead to bad experiences for some students and they are not something most people have to do in the course of their daily living. Unfortunately, public speaking tends to get a bad rap because some junior high and high school teachers require students to memorize speeches which can lead to some bad experiences in front of an audience for a student.

Vocal Aspects of Speech Delivery

There are six aspects of vocal delivery a speaker utilizes that influence an audience's interpretation of the speaker's message. 1. Pitch is the highness or lowness of a speaker's voice. It is the natural upward and downward movement that happens when we speak – the melody. Pitch is a learned activity. When you were born, you didn't have pitch but you learned it from the significant people in your life. When your mom or dad talked "baby talk" to you – all that "ga, ga, goo, goo" stuff – they spoke using a variety of pitches. Your parent used quiet soft tones to bring about a soothing, calm response from you or happy, lively tones to bring about a smile or coo from you. As a baby you learned to mimic the melodies you heard from your parents. This is why family members often sound alike in their speech tones and patterns – children mimic those that they are around the most. For instance, if you heard my mom, and then myself on the phone, we sound exactly alike! If you were born without the ability to hear, you couldn't learn pitch which is why a deaf person who has learned to speak tends to sound monotone – they can't mimic because they can't hear. When it comes to public speaking, don't try to fight your natural pitch by sounding more "professional" or more "in charge." Let your natural melody flow as you deliver a presentation. 2. Rate is how fast or slow you speak when delivering a speech. A common problem of nervous public speakers is speaking too quickly or feeling like you are rushing through a speech which can lead to a cotton mouth feeling. To counter act rushing the presentation, have a bottle of water on hand and take a drink when you feel like you are rushing – this should slow you down. Likewise, concentrating too much on slowing down can cause you to drag your presentation. Try to speak at a natural rate when you are delivering your presentation. 3. Pauses are intended silences during a speech. In conversation, we naturally pause at the end of sentences and at the end of a thought. We should keep up the same pausing pattern in our public speaking that we use in our natural conversation. We can also use pauses to control an audience that might not be paying attention to the presentation. By taking a little bit longer pause than normal, an audience member will notice the silence and usually stop chatting, whispering, or being disrespectful. 4. Volume is the relative loudness of your voice as you deliver a presentation. It shouldn't come as much of a surprise that you need to match your volume to the size of the room you are speaking in. You should also pay attention to your audience – audience members are great about telling you when they can't hear. They will tend to lean forward or look around confused if you are too quiet. They may even make verbal comments like "What did she say?" or "Can you hear him?" When you see or hear this happening in your audience, speak louder. 5. Enunciation is the pronunciation and articulation of words in your speech. Each word is composed of syllables which are the little parts of each word that combine together to make a particular sound. The word "sugar" is composed of two syllables – "Shu" and "gar." When we don't pronounce each syllable in a word, we sound mush-mouthed and don't sound clear to an audience. As you give a presentation, concentrate on speaking very clearly and using your entire mouth to form each word. Most of us in our daily conversation are pretty sloppy in our talk – we rarely use our entire mouth to converse. In public speaking it is essential to use your entire mouth, speaking extremely clearly while making sure you say each syllable.

6. Fluency is the smoothness of your vocal delivery. Fluency is the flow of your words in the delivery of your speech. You should strive for a smooth delivery in your presentation but if your tongue gets tripped up, don't panic. Everyone gets tripped up at one point or another – even professional actors. That's why there are out-takes on movies! We all stumble over unfamiliar or new words or even old words we've said a thousand times. The trick is to not make a big deal out of the flub when it happens. Just maintain your professional tone and keep going. The biggest way to prevent stumbling over your words is to practice, practice, practice your presentation so your words are as natural sounding to you as possible. Bodily Aspects of Speech Delivery There are four aspects of a speaker's body which impact an audience's interpretation of the speaker's message. 1. Gestures are movements of the speaker's head, arms, and hands. When you watch a great public speaker, you will notice that their entire body is into the presentation. They use their entire body to deliver the message – their arms gesture, their fingers point or accent important words, and their head even nods when they are talking about something important. Most people

think of a podium as wonderful piece of furniture to have on hand when they give a presentation – usually, because it gives the speaker someplace to hide behind! A podium is designed for one thing and one thing only – to hold your notes. It is not meant to support your weight, to be leaned on, or to death grip with your hands. If you hang onto a podium or death grip it out of fear, you will not be able to gesture and you will simply be a talking head. Most of us gesture naturally in our daily conversation. Many of us are accused of talking with our hands. In fact, if you are asked to sit on your hands and have a conversation with someone, you will probably compensate for the lack of arm/hand gestures by nodding your head or shrugging your shoulders more than normal! If you have a podium to speak at, set your notes on the podium and take one step back from it so you can't hang onto it. This will help you to gesture naturally and you won't hang onto the podium. If you hold your notes in your hand, avoid gesturing with the notes because your audience will logically follow the notes if you wave them around. 2. Facial expressions are movements of the eyes, mouth, chin, etc. The best piece of advice about facial expressions is to make them match your subject. If your speaking about a serious subject, use a serious facial expression but if you are speaking about something funny, go ahead and smile or even laugh. You can ruin a serious presentation by laughing during it and you can ruin a light hearted speech by never cracking a smile. This is a good time to mention humor. Most of us love a good joke but few of us are genuinely funny by nature – just think about how few really great comedians there are in the world. You can certainly use humor in a presentation but if you are not naturally a funny person, don't go there because the audience will know if you are faking it. Likewise, if you are going to use humor, the humor should match the subject you are talking about. In other words, if you are going to use "Why did the chicken cross the road?" you better be speaking about chickens, roads, or what's on the other side of the road for the rest of the speech. The worst thing you can do is to deliver a joke at the beginning of a speech which doesn't match the content of your speech because it sets the audience up with an expectation about your presentation which you can't then fulfill. It is never a good idea to deceive an audience because you ruin the trust between a speaker and the audience. 3. Eye contact is sustained, meaningful contact with the eyes of audience members. This is the top reason most people hate public speaking – the thought of people looking at you and all the eyes on you is probably the most difficult part of public speaking. There are a whole lot of ways that people will tell you to get around the eye contact issue. Some of the most common myths about eye contact include: Look only at the back wall in the room, never at the people in the audience. The trouble with this approach is that you completely ignore the audience which makes audience members feel unconnected to the speaker. Pick three spots and only look at those three spots in the room. The trouble with this approach is that this takes a whole lot of work – you have to remember where your three spots are and where to look next. The audience will feel like you are watching a tennis match instead of looking like at them. Look only at the audience member's foreheads – not at their eyes. Have you ever tried to focus on someone's forehead? Unless there is some sort of strange growth on a forehead, we don't focus on this area of a person's head – we look in them in the eye. Look only at the audience member's chest – not at their eyes. Okay, in today's world, focusing on a woman's chest could get you slapped or thrown in jail so this one is just ridiculous. And, my personal favorites...think of your audience in their underwear or imagine your audience naked. The idea behind these is that by imagining them in these states, you should realize that everyone is the same. My perspective is that if you are imagining a room full of people naked or in their underwear, what is your speech about? Wouldn't it be more productive of you to focus on your presentation instead of what the audience is or isn't wearing? So, if you can't use any of these to survive the eye contact portion of public speaking, how do you survive it? I think the best way to survive eye contact is to understand audience members because they are who you should be making eye contact with. First, audiences are made up of unique individuals – they are not a homogeneous body where everybody is the same. If you understand who is in your audience, public speaking is not nearly as intimidating. Luckily, there are some common types of people who are usually present in every audience. If I were going to speak to 25 people, there are a variety of personalities that would be in the room. Research shows that there will be at least three to five of the 25 who will be clock watchers – meaning they will look at their watch the entire time I am giving the speech. When I give the speech, my ego will react negatively with a clock watcher because I will say to myself "Am I speaking too long?" The reality is the clock watcher is just that, a clock watcher. They may be worried about where they have to be next and not even focused on how long I've been talking. Along with clock watchers, I'm also going to see several people doodling. Doodlers are great but as a speaker, I may find them distracting with my ego questioning "What are they writing? Is it about me?" Research shows doodlers pay better attention than non-doodlers in an audience. They are just adept at multi-tasking so it's not that they are writing cartoon images of me as the speaker. Along with doodlers will be some people who are sleeping. My ego will question whether I am so boring that I am putting people to sleep but the reality may be that those people may not feel well or they had a late night the night before because they work two jobs. This has nothing to do with me or my speech but my ego makes me question it. There will also be a group of people who will just not care about what I am saying. It really has nothing to do with me – it may be that they are distracted or worried about something that happened at home. Unfortunately, my ego works against me when I look out at the audience and I see all of these people not paying 100% attention to me – I get more nervous. So what should I do? Well, I should look for the friendly eyed people in my audience to start my presentation with. They will be there along with the doodlers and clock watchers, sleepers and those that don't care. If I start with the friendly eyes, I can then work out to others in the audiences. If I can look around the room and label the audience members as I go, it empowers me as the speaker and keeps my ego in check. When I feel my ego starting to question my audience, I can go back to the friendly eyes for reassurance that I am doing okay. By looking audience members directly in the eye as much as possible, I validate the audience – they feel connected to me as a speaker and I show them how I value their presence. So, sustained and meaningful eye contact is essential for successful public speaking. 4. Movement is where the speaker's entire body moves. If you can avoid it, don't let yourself be trapped behind a podium or in one area. When you watch a really great speaker, you'll see that they are almost never trapped behind something. They move around the room as they talk and that may mean they are down the aisle or all across the front of the room. The biggest place you can see this happen is by attending a newly constructed church. Most new churches are constructed to allow for personal interaction between a minister and the congregation which is different than most old churches where the minister or priest is isolated in a pulpit that is probably higher than everyone else in the room (giving the minister/priest the appearance of being closer to God than the congregation). Writing Your Outline: The Informative Organizational Patterns There are three major components to any presentation: the introduction, the body, and the conclusion. The natural inclination would be to start writing a presentation with the introduction since this section comes first. However, I recommend that you start writing the body first because the body will determine what goes into the introduction and conclusion. The Body The body is the heart of the speech – it takes the longest to get through. In an eight minute speech, the body is between six and seven minutes long. It is composed of three sections: main points, sub-points, and evidence. The body of an informative speech on the legislative process might look like this:Body: I. Drafting the bill A. Sub-point B. Sub-point 1. Evidence 2. Evidence II. Committee hearings A. Sub-point 1. Evidence B. Sub-point C. Sub-point III. Floor debate on the bill A. Sub-point B. Sub-point C. Sub-point Main points are the major ideas you want to discuss about your subject. In the sample above it would include Drafting the bill, Committee hearings, and Floor debate on the bill. When it comes to choosing a subject, never chose to talk about something you have no passion for. Always choose to speak about something you have experience or expertise with because it makes your presentation much more interesting to the audience – you will transfer your passion about the subject matter to them! I recommend that you stick with three major main points or aspects of your subject to talk about. The human brain naturally chunks memory into sequences of threes so three main points will be easier for you to remember (think about the sequence in your telephone number – this is why your phone number is in sequences of three and then a four). Main points are composed of a combination of sub-points and evidence. Sub-points are your ideas or personal knowledge about the main point you are discussing. This could be a description of your experience or expertise on the subject. In the sample above, the personal expertise of the speaker could be something they have seen on a trip – on a tour of our nation's capital to see floor debate in action. Evidence is the information that you quote or summarize from another source about the main point. This means that you will need to research your subject thoroughly to obtain quality information to quote or summarize in your presentation. Since the speaker in the example above is not a legislator, they would need to research the process and cite the research findings in the presentation.

CHAPTER SEVENTEEN

FEARLESS SPEAKING

The goal of this book is to change your life. To paraphrase a well-known saying: Today is the first day of the rest of your life as someone who used to have public speaking anxiety. You're about to conquer a fear that has diminished your speaking pleasure, delayed your professional advancement, or disturbed your peace of mind. It may have been a nagging worry for years that you've finally decided to face, once and for all. Or perhaps your speech fright only revealed itself recently. Some of the clients I work with, for instance, are senior executives who've been speaking in public comfortably for decades, yet they've suddenly lost their self-confidence. I don't take these clients back to their childhoods to figure out why they're anxious about speaking in public. Instead, we identify how their reluctance to speak is manifesting itself now, in the present. Once we have that information, we can work on reducing their fears and building their self-confidence along with their speaking skills.That's exactly what this book will do for you. And you're going to get started right now. Overcoming speaking anxiety truly is something that will change your life, so why wait? Your new understanding and confidence will open up opportunities for you and show you the enjoyment you've been missing. Just how powerful will eliminating public speaking fear be for you? The brief form below will help you decide. It's the first of many hands-on exercises for reducing speech anxiety that you'll find in Fearless Speaking.

EXERCISE 1-1 OVERCOMING SPEAKING ANXIETY WILL CHANGE YOUR LIFE List three ways that not reducing but eliminating public speaking anxiety will positively impact your personal life and career: 1. ____

2____

3. ____

THE BEST METHOD FOR OVERCOMING YOUR SPEAKING FEAR Obviously, the three items you just listed are important for your overall peace of mind and enjoyment of public speaking. Now, how will you actually achieve those positive developments? You probably won't be surprised to hear that the best way to overcome stage fright and reach your speaking goals is to learn a few techniques from the theater. Actors are the world's best speakers despite speaking anxiety. Did you know, for instance, that these performers suffer from stage fright as much as anyone? The difference between actors and everyone else is that stage acting teaches them the most efficient ways for overcoming their speaking fear.

You don't need to suddenly become an actor to benefit from these techniques yourself. I do, however, use the time-tested tools and techniques of the theater with people from all walks of life because I know they produce results. I recognized this truth years ago when I began working with business executives and other professionals. After all, effective performance is the core of all good speaking— whether it's in a theater, a boardroom, a meeting, or at the conference you're attending. Another thing that actors understand is that talking about performance is helpful only in the beginning phases of rehearsal. After that it's time for action. That's why at each stage of helping people cope with their speech fear, I include actionable exercises to reduce apprehension while boosting my clients' skills and confidence. Some of these exercises are designed to change thinking patterns (a process known as "cognitive restructuring"). Others are based in emotional response. Some feature positive visualization, while others are concerned with staying focused and present for audiences. Whichever exercises I'm using, however, my approach always includes dealing with the body's response to stage fright. That's because fear of public speaking nearly always produces a predictable physical reaction. The exercises you'll find throughout Fearless Speaking come directly from the approach and techniques I use in my work in Boston. Here's the great news about the speaking jitters you experience: this level of mental and physical activation is perfectly natural and even beneficial. Without those butterflies in your stomach, you might become too laid-back and bland, without any of the edge or energy that makes you exciting as a speaker. It's only when the balance tips too far toward anxiety that the normal level of nervousness that otherwise helps you, morphs into debilitating fear. NERVOUSNESS IS NORMAL, BUT FEAR MAKES YOU IRRATIONAL Don't believe that those butterflies can be helpful? Then ask yourself this question: Do you know anyone who doesn't get at least a little nervous before speaking in public? I don't. I've been performing on stage since I was nine years old (my first performance was to 1,500 people). And I still get those butterflies before speaking to groups, and a high-stakes speech or presentation will sometimes make me have trouble sleeping the night before. Those reactions are normal and fairly universal. As I said earlier, stage performers undergo all of this, too. The difference is the degree of the reaction they experience. Getting slightly nervous is helpful because it psyches you up for the "big game." But deep-seated fear or a gnawing anxiety is likely to push you over into irrational thinking. Below are four common misconceptions about public speaking that reflect such thinking. Each of them is an unreasonable conclusion, or what I call a fiction. You should learn to recognize them and send them on their way without you! FOUR FICTIONS ABOUT PUBLIC SPEAKING Fiction #1: Public speaking is dangerous. This is a particularly widespread and damaging myth. Not only are audience members not your enemy; but even a failed presentation will rarely result in your being fired, demoted, or even seriously compromised in your job. Speaking isn't a perilous adventure on the order of any of the things that should really scare you, no matter how hard you try to make it so. Remember, a diamond is formed by pressure, and only afterwards is it polished. If you find speaking in public challenging, that means it's a golden opportunity for you to shine. Fiction #2: Nervousness will make your performance worse. There is no reliable link between feeling anxious and giving a bad performance. At least in all my years helping speakers I've never found one. Quite to the contrary, there are many stories from business and the professions, when someone will speak and then say to a colleague, "I know I was horrible . . . I was so nervous." And the other person will respond: "Really? You looked fine to me." Fiction #3: Everyone will see how nervous you are. And once they do, the entire audience will doubt your credibility! This is non-sense. Most nervousness isn't visible to others because it's internal. And if people do see you're nervous, they'll most likely have the normal reaction, which is to sympathize with you. Since audience members feel good when you're succeeding and embarrassed when you're failing, they're actually on your side and want you to do well. Fiction #4: You have to be an excellent speaker. Who says so? If you're a motivational speaker by profession perhaps that's so, but otherwise it isn't true. The belief that you have to be "excellent" is often a hindrance to effective public speaking because it confuses polish for true communication. When you speak to people (who almost always want to be in the audience), your job is to connect with them and give them something of value. Your task isn't to be slick, charismatic, or a stand-up comic. So concern yourself instead with being honest and trustworthy. And if you happen to give a lackluster presentation, so what? Failure can be the best of teachers, since you'll want to do that much better the next time. DEVELOPING A POSITIVE MINDSET Now that you've brought to light this quartet of damaging public speaking fictions, it's time to banish them by stepping from this negative territory into a more positive mindset. The following exercise is an excellent one for getting your thinking headed in that direction. Rather than "trying to be an excellent speaker" (as we saw above), this activity will bring you more in touch with the positive attributes you already have to offer listeners. Remember, regardless of whether you succeed or fail in a particular presentation, your performance doesn't change who you are as a person. There's an excellent reason, for instance, why you were asked to speak in front of that audience: you're exactly the right person for the job! Why not remind yourself of that fact? The exercise on the next page entitled "Your Public Speaking Strengths" is designed to help you do so. This exercise has two parts. In the first part, you'll fill out an inventory of your attributes as a speaker. Don't be shy; be honest. This is your opportunity to reacquaint yourself with all the good things you have going for you as a presenter. It's easy to lose sight of those valuable skills once you become focused on your anxiety instead of your abilities. So for the next few minutes, blow your own trumpet . . . I won't tell!

EXERCISE 1-2 YOUR PUBLIC SPEAKING STRENGTHS List your strengths as an oral communicator. When you're with people you feel comfortable around, what makes them listen to you? Do they appreciate your intelligence, sense of humor, passion, playfulness, kindness, quirkiness, or other traits? What assets help you when you speak to others? List your physical attributes, vocal qualities, energy, listening skills, creativity, subject matter expertise, and any other strength that helps you communicate with people.

____

____

____

____

____

____

EXERCISE 1-3 TALKING ABOUT YOUR STRENGTHS Good! Now for the follow-through—because this is a book about better public speaking, after all. Take a few minutes to look over your list on the previous page. Once you've become familiar with it, talk on this subject for between two and five minutes. In other words, your topic is "My Public Speaking Strengths." Use your notes if you like. Imagine that you're interviewing for a fabulous job and the interviewer says, "We're quite interested in your oral communication skills. In fact, it's the only thing we're interested in. So tell us what makes you an effective communicator." Feel free to record your talk on audio or videotape it. Writing down your attributes as a speaker is a down payment on your willingness to succeed at public speaking. But actually talking about good communication will give you practice in speaking freely and frequently, and get you closer to sealing the deal. So go for it

THE BENEFITS OF STAGE FRIGHT If your response to the above heading is, "There are actually benefits to stage fright?" then my answer is: You'd better believe it! Here's why: The anxiety you feel about important events in your life actually prepares you for challenging or dangerous situations. But as you saw in Fiction #1, public speaking isn't dangerous—you just perceive it that way if you have anxiety about speaking in public. Your fearful response is, therefore, a beneficial reaction that helps build up your skills so that you can succeed in front of an audience. As I said earlier, the key is finding a balance between your ordinary, beneficial nervousness, and actual anxiety that's more harmful than productive.

Here are three specific ways that your "helpful" stage fright is a positive reaction: 3 WAYS STAGE FRIGHT IS HELPFUL TO YOU 1. It shows you care about your audience. 2. It gets you ready for peak performance. 3. It's a source of energy you can channel positively. UNDERSTANDING YOUR PERSONAL RESPONSE Now that you realize stage fright can be a positive reaction, you're ready to understand more closely your specific response to speaking fear. The step after that, later in this chapter, will be matching your reaction with the best technique to deal with that particular response. Ready? Please turn to the exercise on the next page.

EXERCISE 1-4 UNDERSTANDING SPEAKING FEAR Please complete the sections below concerning the eight causes of speech anxiety. Answer the questions honestly and candidly. Your answers will help you know whether you have speaking fear, and identify the type of fear response(s) you experience. Knowing this information will help you zero in on the fear reduction technique best suited to your situation. Feel free to answer, "Yes" to more than one of the eight causes. But once you've completed the entire exercise, go back and circle the name of the response that is strongest for you. It will be helpful for you to know this information when you get to the Fear Reduction Techniques shown later in this chapter.1 Learned Response. Are you still influenced by a negative public speaking or performance situation that happened to you in the past? Did something "teach" you that public appearances are unpleasant, risky, or even dangerous? Have you been afraid to get up in front of others since then? Yes, I have a learned response. _____ No, I can't think of anything like that. _____ Maybe. There's something that might apply. _____ Please explain:

____

____

____

____

____

____

____

Anticipatory Anxiety. Does the thought of giving a speech or presentation cause you excessive anxiety beforehand? Do you worry constantly about the upcoming speaking situation, lose sleep, have no appetite, or fixate on what's coming? Yes, I experience excessive anticipation. _____ No, I don't worry excessively. _____ Somewhat. _____ Describe what you go through:

____

____

____

Mindreading. Do you believe you know what your audience is thinking? Can you "hear" them in your own mind challenging and criticizing you? Are you certain that their facial expressions reveal their true feelings toward you? Yes, I think I know what people are thinking. _____ No, I usually leave my crystal ball at home. _____ I respond like that in some situations. _____ Share your thoughts with yourself now:

Fear of Appearing Nervous. Is your greatest fear that everyone will see how nervous you are? In other words, do you think, "If I appear truly nervous, everyone will realize I don't know what I'm talking about!" Is this your big concern? Yes, I'm afraid of appearing nervous. _____ No, I don't think like that when I'm presenting. _____ I do worry about that at times. _____ Please explain:

Fear of Going Blank. Are you afraid that nervousness and anxiety will make you forget everything you're supposed to say? Do you picture yourself having a brain freeze? Are you convinced you'll be unable to say anything or that you'll forget key parts of your message? Yes, I'm constantly afraid I'll lose my train of thought. _____ No, that isn't my concern. _____ I sometimes have that response. _____ Please explain these feelings:

Lack of Skills. Are you convinced that you simply lack talent as a public speaker and shouldn't be up there? Are you afraid that you'll be "found out" and your secret will no longer be safe? Yes, I believe deep down that I'm just not a _____ good speaker. No, I can't say I feel like that. _____ Certain aspects of my speaking skills do concern me. _____ Explain here:

Physical Reaction. Is your biggest problem the physical responses you have when you speak in front of others? Is your principal complaint dry mouth, pounding heart, gastrointestinal distress, racing pulse, sweating, shaky voice, gasping for breath, or other symptoms? Absolutely! This is my biggest problem. _____ No, physical distress isn't the worst thing I go through. _____ I do experience some physical discomfort. _____ Please explain what you feel physically if this is a source of discomfort:

Performance Orientation. Is your principal concern that you have to be an excellent speaker? Do you compare yourself to other speakers, telling yourself you have to come up to their level? Is your skill in performance your major concern? Yes, I need to be excellent and don't think I am. _____ No, I'm focused on my message not my performance. _____ I do sometimes compare myself with others. _____ Please explain:

____

____

____

____

____

____

Well done! Now that you've identified possible anxiety responses, you can focus on the technique best suited to deal with that particular response. Exercise 1-5 on "Types of Fear Reduction Techniques" on the next page shows you how to do that. Match the principal speaking fear you just identified (all eight are listed in the left-hand column) with the fear reduction techniques in the right column. Each of these techniques will be explained in further detail later in the book. Those are the techniques you can work closely with for maximum results!

Before you start planning your presentation, find out from the organizers how much time you have and what format they envision for your talk. Will you be part of a panel or will you be speaking alone? Will you be in a regular session or are you the dinner speaker? Do you have 15 minutes or an hour? Do they prefer to leave time for questions? I f yes, does that come out of the allocated time you have been quoted? It is important to know what is expected of you so you can be well prepared and not have to scramble last minute to readjust your talk due to unanticipated logistics.

Public Speaking Can Drastically Improve Your Life

Public speaking is one of the best ways I know to help you improve your life and career.

In addition to helping you stand out as a leader in your career, public speaking has an impact on everything you think, feel and do. The benefits transcend your career and will leak into your personal life.

I know because the lessons I have learned through public speaking have helped me become more social, confident and engaging. In this article, I want to share with you the 5 biggest ways public speaking can drastically improve your life

1) You Learn to Empathize:

The best public speakers know that every part of their speech is for the benefit of their audience. One of the biggest mistakes speakers make is centering their focus on themselves. You can always spot a speaker whose focus is on making himself look more intelligent or credible. These types of speakers make the audience uncomfortable and unsatisfied because of a lack of authenticity. The best speakers share stories to connect with their audiences as well as inspire and entertain.

To shift the focus from you to your audience, I want to take you through an exercise that has been very beneficial to me as a speaker.

Step 1. Picture the most important person in your life. This may be a sibling, a parent or a spouse.

Step 2. In your mind, place that treasured person in the third row of your audience.

Step 3. What is the main takeaway you want that person to receive from your speech? (Example: "friends are the family you choose", "follow your dreams", "don't eat the yellow snow", etc.)

Step 4. Condense that message into 10 words or less.

Step 5. Build your entire speech around that message.

This exercise helps you speak to your audience as if everyone was your closest friend, parent or sibling. When this practice leaks into the day to day conversations at work, you start to notice people are more engaged when you place a deeper value on them.

2) You Learn to Control Your Thoughts and Emotions:

Public speaking will give you awareness of what is going on between your ears. It will force you to notice your internal thoughts and inner critic. The best presenters still get nervous before getting on stage, they just know how to control their thoughts in order to turn nervousness into excitement. To take a quote from Buddha "all that we are is a result of what we have thought." Right before getting up to speak in front of an audience, it is perfectly natural to get butterflies. The way you learn to control your thoughts and emotions is seen in the way you interpret these butterflies. By changing the pattern in your head from "I'm sick to my stomach with nervousness" to "I'm churning with excitement" you will manage your nerves and give presentations from a place of joy rather than fear.

Public speaking will also help you manage your emotions by teaching you to let things go. The projector will fail sometimes, you will forget a major point you wanted to make, your microphone will screech as you try to speak into it. The best way to deal with this is to take a deep breath and just let go. You learn to generate a positive state from within and be positive and insightful. Or you learn to be like a duck "calm on the surface but paddling like crazy underneath."

As the concentration camp survivor Viktor Frankl puts it "between stimulus and response, there is an empty space where we may choose how to react." In everyday life, things happen to us that are outside of our circle of influence and we may spill coffee on our work clothes or our co-workers say something off-putting. It is by learning to control the way we interpret and respond to these situations that we can free ourselves from everyday distress.

3) You Improve Your Life by Learning from Failure:

I have given more speeches than I can count and some have been excruciating. My freshman year of college, I had to give a simple presentation about the United States to the international club. Thinking this would be easy, I went out that night and did not start to prepare for my presentation until 11PM. I left the library that morning, bleary-eyed and exhausted as the sun was rising. I skipped breakfast – except for a quick cup of coffee – and gave my speech an hour later. Jittery and incoherent, I found that my jokes were misinterpreted, my information was scattered and the question and answer period was dreadful. From this painful experience, I learned to always get a full nights rest before a presentation. My next presentation, with a full nights rest and a lot less caffeine, received excellent reviews.

Your life goes through cycles of ups and downs – victory and loss. One day you get a promotion and the next day you miss an important meeting. It is by picking ourselves up after falling and learning from failure that we find the greatest success.

4) You Learn to Apply Lessons from Public Speaking to Other Skills:

At the Magnetic Delivery Bootcamp, people are usually outside of their comfort zone when they are asked to speak in front of audiences. As the day progresses and they gain more hands-on practice and learn more about public speaking, they eventually cross a threshold and gain more confidence. This results in momentum and gives them faster results throughout the day because they are focused on their progress rather than their anxiety.

For you, the trick is to start where you're a little bit uncomfortable and continually push your limits, eventually presenting to larger audiences, speaking off the cuff or volunteering for projects involving presentations at work. Once you get the hang of it, you will start to enjoy the process and love the results, continually striving to improve your communication.

Like basketball, pottery or cooking, public speaking is a skill that is developed with time and practice. Few people are naturally comfortable in front of large audiences just as few people can create a clay masterpiece. With the right attitude, help from a mentor and commitment to improving your abilities you will gain a confidence that people are amazed by.

5) Public Speaking Helps you Navigate the World:

We live in a world that is, obviously, dominated by humans. Business, politics, marriage and every other major part of our lives require communication. As one of the great communicators of our time, Tony Robbins puts it "the quality of your communication determines the quality of your life." Public speaking – connecting and communicating with large groups of people – gives you a skill set and confidence that overflows into every aspect of your life.

In learning to effectively give a speech, you also improve the quality of every interaction you have, which magnifies your character and makes you a more engaging person. In public speaking, you learn to present yourself with strong body language, sincere tonality, and engaging eye contact. This enriches your everyday interactions and results in higher quality business relationships, friendships and marriages.

I have been to 22 different countries throughout Asia, Africa, South America and Europe and a big insight I have gained from my experiences has been that communication makes life so much easier. In many of the countries I have been to, English is taught as a second language and having the confidence to smile and say "where is the nearest bathroom?" has been incredibly useful. In addition, many of the conversations I have started while abroad have led to incredible experiences and meaningful friendships.

Public speaking is one of the most powerful skills you can develop because it gives you a confidence that improves every area of your life. I challenge you to take the next step with your public speaking skills and join the local Toastmasters, enroll in a speaking course or volunteer to give a presentation at work. The benefits are guaranteed to improve your long-term business, career and relationship success.

Advantages Of Public Relations

In recent years, we have seen a significant shift from traditional marketing to an integrated marketing approach. As an important aspect of integrated marketing communication, Public Relations or widely known as PR enables businesses to reinforce their advertising message effectively and in an authentic manner. Public relations is a powerful management tool for companies to reach their business objectives and build their image and presence. However, public relations and publicity is often underutilised and neglected as companies are unsure about what PR is and what it can do.

Here are 5 advantages of PR for you to consider:

1. Increase your brand's credibility

Publicity through public relations gives credibility to your business as the content is more authentic and informative. Studies indicate that PR gives more visibility and credibility among the consumer market than advertising which is perceived as more promotional.

2. Attract your target market

PR allows a much easier approach to retaining and attracting a target market. A well-written article on your product/service offerings in the magazine can be much more attractive and impact compared to an advertisement in that same magazine. Further, by utilising multiple media sources from a PR agency, you can effectively communicate your key messages and help you get a step closer to achieving your company goals.

3. Provide added value

PR can provide a unique touch point and add value to your product offering that can help differentiate you among your competitors and put you at the forefront of your particular industry. Further, PR can add value through increasing visibility of your products and services, personalise your brand, raise your profile, build strong relationships, manage your reputation, assist with your sales process and add value to your own clients through case studies. Overall, it is a win-win scenario.

4. Short and long-term lead generation

Media placements through PR are a form of long-term placement as initially you are likely to be exposed to large amount of leads. But as time goes on you will notice that there is a still a lead from just one media mention. Generating leads will come across frequently as businesses and customers stagger on PR.

5. Build your brand image

People often assume that PR is all about promoting an item or a special offer. This is a misconception as PR drives your entire business towards growth and greater yield of success. When done right, PR can create a more positive brand image in the mind of your consumers that provides an alley way to better engagement for your company. A great brand image is a business investment that can't be bought and will provide value to your brand and your customer as it helps shape all aspects of your business as a whole.

Taurus is an award-winning integrated marketing agency. With our extensive experience and strong relationship with the media, we are dedicated to delivering smart communications strategies which generate momentum and initiative behind our clients to help your companies reach new heights!

9 798885 309486

Printed by Libri Plureos GmbH in Hamburg,
Germany